Blue-Collar Leadership® & Culture

The 5 Components for Building High Performance Teams

Mack Story

DEDICATION

To those rare, high impact leaders who are willing to
intentionally challenge their own thinking as they strive
to lead their teams to the next level and beyond.

CONTENTS

ACKNOWLEDGMENTS

I would like to acknowledge the late S. Truett Cathy, Chick-fil-A® Founder, Jimmy Collins, Chick-fil-A® President and COO (Ret.), Dee Ann Turner, Chick-fil-A® VP of Talent (Ret.), and Bob Chapman, Barry-Wehmiller CEO. All of them have inspired me.

Each of these leaders and their teams created and sustained exceptional cultures within their respective industries. Their cultures have been and continue to be the competitive advantage that separate their organizations from their competition.

Jimmy Collins has been a friend and mentor since I first met him on June 18, 2015. I'm extremely grateful for the hours he has invested in me, for the lunches we've shared together, for the many stories he shared about his nearly 33 years creating the Chick-fil-A® culture with Truett Cathy from startup in 1967 to $1 billion in annual sales by 2001, for inviting me into his home to record several episodes with him as a guest on my Blue-Collar Leadership® Podcast, and for all of the support and encouragement he has given me and my wife, Ria Story, as we've built our Blue-Collar Leadership® brand. The high impact culture that Jimmy Collins and Truett Cathy established during those first 33 years together produced $10.5 billion in annual sales in 2018.

That didn't happen by accident; it happened by design.

CULTURE
COUNTS

1

THE COST OF CULTURE

THE 3 DILEMMAS:
ENGAGEMENT, RETENTION, AND TURNOVER

"When trust goes down, speed will also go down and costs will go up. When trust goes up, speed will also go up and costs will go down." ~ Stephen M. R. Covey

I've logged well over 11,000 hours leading leaders and their blue-collar teams through process improvement, organizational change, and cultural transformation. I've learned a lot. But, two things were obvious from the start:
1) Every team member wants a great leader.
2) Every leader wants great team members.

I discovered many leaders were frustrated because they had disengaged team members. Employee engagement is not only the key to increasing retention, productivity, profitability, and teamwork, but it's also the key to reducing turnover, costs, and frustrations. Numerous research studies reveal only 30-35% of employees consider themselves engaged.

As a result, many leaders are facing three costly dilemmas: engagement, retention, and turnover.

THE ENGAGEMENT DILEMMA:
Employee engagement starts with engaged leadership. Disengaged employees are a symptom of disengaged leaders at one or more levels in your

organization. In fact, research studies show employees are 40% more productive if they *want* to follow their leader compared to those who feel they *have* to follow their leader. In other words, the level of engagement below is determined by the level of engagement above.

Leadership development, or the lack of it, at every level determines morale, engagement, turnover, productivity, communication, teamwork, and how your customers will be served. Unfortunately, many people are over-managed and under-led.

People who are led well become highly engaged.

People who are over-managed become disengaged.

Leadership development is the key to transforming the culture of your organization, improving your team's results, and reducing costs in all areas.

THE RETENTION DILEMMA:

The competition wants more than your customers. Have you considered there are two types of competition? 1) Those in the same industry who want to steal your customers; and 2) Those who may or may not be in the same industry who want to steal your people.

A leader's ability to attract and retain high performance employees is a crucial factor for organizational success. Employees who are disengaged are far more likely to change jobs and even change industries because disengagement leads to dissatisfaction.

Minimizing employee turnover by increasing engagement through leadership development is critical to improving your bottom line.

High performance team members and managers are looking for more than a good salary. They are seeking growth and development opportunities that will help them become more successful personally and professionally. As Heather Huhman stated, "87% of managers wish they had more training before becoming a manager." High impact leaders understand they must offer more development opportunities in order to become the sought after employer of choice in their industry and in their area of operation.

THE TURNOVER DILEMMA:

Are you tired of hiring, then firing? Employees are primarily interviewed, selected, and hired based on their competency. In this case, competency means a leader believes the candidate has the required skillset, technical knowledge, and ability to perform the task or job.

However, most employees are terminated based on character. Character relates to who we are and how we do what we do. It's the "soft" skills, such as attitude, work ethic, integrity, behavior, and how we work with others.

In other words, employees are hired for what they know, but fired for who they are. Performance problems are almost exclusively a character issue. According to Daniel Goleman, "90% of our results as individuals and organizations is determined by character." However, most organizational training and development is focused on improving competency, not character.

If your team isn't engaged, you're likely dealing with some level of frustration, resistance, confusion, anxiety, and stagnation. It doesn't have to be this way.

"Imagine the personal and organizational cost of failing to fully engage the passion, talent, and intelligence of the workforce. It is far greater than all taxes, interest charges, and labor costs put together."
~ Stephen R. Covey

2

THE FOUNDATION OF CULTURE

THE ORGANIZATIONAL CULTURE WILL BE DETERMINED BY THE LEADER'S VALUES

"Greatness is achieved by using resources to help people; not using people as a resource."
~ Captain L. David Marquet, U. S. Navy

Merriam-Webster defines culture as, "the set of shared attitudes, values, goals, and practices that characterizes an institution or organization."

"Values" is the key word because your values are the underlying foundation which fuel your thoughts. Thoughts produce your emotions which influence your choices. Choices lead to your results which determine your circumstances. The culture of an organization can be traced back to a single root cause: the top leader's values.

Values on the inside are revealed as character traits on the outside. I'm reminded of the words of Andy Stanley, "Character is personal, but it's not private." The culture of an organization isn't private either. The people on the inside are always talking about it to people on the outside.

Because values are revealed outwardly as character, the collective character of everyone in an organization is what is commonly referred to as the "culture" of the organization. Organizational culture is simply a reflection of the combined character of all of the people within the organization. As Gruenter and Whitaker pointed out, "The culture of any organization is shaped by the worst behavior the leader is willing to tolerate."

Culture equals character. Character equals culture.

High impact leaders understand the culture of an organization affects everything else – and culture starts with them. Before a leader can change their culture, they must change their values. Why? Because the leader's current values are what created the current culture.

High impact leaders know it doesn't cost anything to care for their team members. They also know it costs a lot when they don't.

As a leader, your character, which is based on your values, will determine your culture. Your character will determine: your ability to build meaningful relationships, whether you build trust or create distrust, what you tolerate, what you expect, what people say about you, who you attract, who you repel, who stays, who goes, and how long they stay before they go.

Michael Josephson said it best, "You don't have to be sick to get better." But, you must have a desire to get better. And ultimately, you must act on that desire.

My wife, Ria, and I had the privilege of joining John C. Maxwell and 150 others in Guatemala in June 2013 to kickoff the "Transformation Begins with Me" cultural transformation initiative across the entire nation. We were privileged to join John and the President of Guatemala at the Presidential Palace for a special celebration as the vision was broadcast live nationally. In just three days, our team conducted four hour development workshops for nearly 20,000 Guatemalan leaders.

When the Guatemalan leaders chose to value cultural transformation, cultural transformation started to occur.

Until a leader values developing their character, they won't develop their character. Until a leader values developing the character of those on their team, they won't develop the character of those on their team. Until a leader values transforming the culture, they won't transform their culture. Until a leader values using resources to develop people, they won't use resources to develop people.

Your values determine your direction.

Relative to developing people, John C. Maxwell made a powerful observation, "Authenticity—This is the foundation for developing people. Servanthood—This is the soul for developing people. Growth—This is the measurement for developing people. Excellence—This is the standard for developing people. Passion—This is the fuel for developing people. Success—This is the purpose for developing people."

When one person gets a little better, the culture gets a little better. When a lot of people get a lot better, the culture gets a lot better. As Lieutenant General George Flynn stated, "Culture equals values plus behavior."

My mission is to help leaders engage the front line to improve the bottom line.[SM] I do this by helping leaders develop the character of everyone on their team from the very top to the very bottom. When it comes to character development, no one should be exempt. We all need it.

Leaders who value developing others attract great people. Leaders who don't develop people struggle to find good people.

It's always easier to compete when you're attracting great people instead of searching for good people.

"Values are not simply posters on a wall.
In order for a culture to be strong, your values
must be clear and your values must be lived."
~ Simon Sinek

3

THE IMPACT OF CULTURE

THOSE WHO WORK THERE WILL DETERMINE WHO WANTS TO WORK THERE

"I think the most important and difficult thing is to create a culture in the organization where leadership is really important. It's important for people in the company to realize that this is a growth-oriented company, and the biggest thing we have to grow here is you, because it's you who will make this company better by your own growth." ~ Jim Blanchard

Listen to the voices of leaders who are losing the labor war:

- "We just can't find any good people."
  As if…there aren't any good or great people.
- "Due to the low unemployment rate, there just aren't any good people left."
  As if…the only people who can be offered a job are those without a job.
- "In today's labor market, those who want to work are already working."
  As if…those who are working at one place can't decide to work at a different place.
- "When we do get good people, they won't stay."
  As if…the problem is always with the people and never with their leaders.

One thing I know about leaders who make these and similar comments is this: Their culture is a competitive disadvantage. Someone else has the advantage and is winning the battle for the good and great people. The good and great people certainly aren't out of work wishing they had a job. They're working someplace else.

Until a leader is aware of the problem, they can't address the problem. In case it's not obvious, the problem is their culture. The leader owns this problem whether they want to or not. Every time I hear these comments, and I hear them a lot, I know I'm talking to a leader who doesn't know what they don't know.

Ria and I hear leaders across varying blue-collar and white-collar industries repeatedly making these comments as we travel across the USA speaking on leadership development. These voices seem to be getting louder and louder. In fact, these voices are an inspiration for this book.

There are many leaders in blue-collar industries needing help. I want to help them stop searching for good people and start attracting great people. The transformation won't happen overnight. However, until it starts happening, it's not going to happen. My intention is to use this book to raise awareness while providing a transformational road map for those leaders who want to make their culture their greatest competitive advantage.

We were speaking in Louisville, KY recently to owners of blue-collar organizations. Afterward, one approached and said, "There isn't a magic pill is there? I think we all hoped there was." I replied, "No sir. There isn't a magic pill or an easy button. This is how you build a high performance team and an exceptional culture that will attract, retain, and support them. There is no other way."

Your culture is always attracting certain types of people and repelling others. Who we are is who we attract. This principle applies to individuals as well as organizations. The culture within your organization is negatively or positively impacting those within the organization, and some who are outside the organization.

The key point is to understand the people inside your organization are constantly providing the most influential type of advertising about your organization and the leaders within it. It's called word of mouth advertising. How your team is feeling inside the organization will determine what they're saying outside the organization.

If what they're saying about their leaders and the organization to others is good, it'll be easier to find good people. If what they're saying is great, it'll be easier to attract great people. But, if what they're saying is bad, finding good people will be hard, if not impossible.

Remember the voices at the start of this chapter? Those leaders had team members who were sharing bad word of mouth advertising about the organization. Unless those leaders choose to change, nothing will change.

Common sense reveals it's easier to win the labor war while attracting great people instead of searching for good people. However, what's common sense isn't always common practice. Often, it takes uncommon sense to act on things that are commonly understood. Creating an organizational culture that will attract and retain great people requires leaders with uncommon sense.

The best led companies aren't impacted by labor shortages because they're consistently attracting the best and the brightest people to their organizations.

"If we lose sight of people, we lose sight of the very purpose of leadership." ~ Tony Dungy

4

BECOMING A
SOUGHT AFTER EMPLOYER

PEOPLE WHO DON'T WORK THERE
WANT TO WORK THERE

*"Leaders set the standard – both by how they lead
and by what they do –they are the guardians of,
and must be held accountable for, the culture."*
~ Charles G. Koch, CEO Koch Industries

I want to set the bar high right from the start as we begin our cultural transformation journey together. To ensure our cultural vision is aligned, let me clarify. Becoming a sought after employer means: Great people who don't work at your organization become aware of and are attracted to your organization, and most importantly, they have a strong desire to work there.

By great people, I mean top talent. By top talent, I mean people who not only have exceptional, well-developed competency (experience, knowledge, abilities), but also people who have exceptional, well-developed character (integrity, humility, trustworthy, responsible).

Sure, good people, and some people who aren't so good, will be attracted as well. But, my goal is to help you develop a culture that attracts great people. When you're attracting great people consistently, it becomes easier to say no to the good people and easy to say no to the people who aren't so good.

Unfortunately, because many leaders of blue-collar organizations haven't focused their energy and resources on developing a high impact culture, they and their support staff find themselves having to take anyone they can get when it's time to fill a position. These are also the organizations that are constantly advertising they're hiring because they can't find good people. And when they do, they don't stay.

If you're struggling to find good people, then attracting good people will sound like a big win. But remember this, a team of good people can't compete effectively with a team of great people. Although, they can easily compete with a team of mediocre people.

My intention is not to help you and your team climb to the middle of the cultural transformation mountain. I want to help you climb to the top.

The mountain will be tall, steep, and challenging at times. To get to the top, you and your team must make the same sacrifices and pay the same price all of those who have stood on the summit have paid. There are no short cuts, but you can increase your speed while traveling on the path to the top.

You get to the top with great people, not good people. Only high performance teams get the view from the top.

You and your team can't climb to the top of the mountain with base camp character. You must be fully aware of the challenge that lies ahead and know where you want to end up. Then, focus on conquering the moment, not the mountain. If you conquer enough moments, you will eventually conquer the mountain.

When it comes to becoming a sought after employer, culture counts. And, it counts a lot. Culture doesn't just happen. It is created, good or bad, by the everyday choices leaders and their teams are making.

Everything I'll share in this book is intended to help you help your organization become a sought after employer that attracts great people and top talent. However, I'm beginning with the end in mind, so I can help you see where I'm trying to lead you.

Becoming a sought after employer is the end result, not the starting point. It's at the top of the cultural transformation mountain, not the bottom.

Everything that follows will help you achieve that result. How long will it take? That's up to you. It depends. For example, if your goal is to swim across a lake and you dive in, you'll get to the other side of the lake much faster than those who simply stand on the bank and stick their toe in the water to see what it feels like.

Your speed will be determined by your investment. By investment, I mean not only time and money, but also your willingness to lead the transformation and change who you are and how you do what you do. It won't happen without you leading the way.

Becoming a sought after employer is not about doing something different. That's easy. It's about becoming something different. That's usually not so easy and is a bit more of a challenge.

What you need to know at this point is this: Before you can become a sought after employer, you must become an employer of choice.

"In a culture of strong character, the people inside the company will feel protected by their leaders and feel that their colleagues have their backs. In a culture of weak character, the people will feel that any protection they have comes primarily from their own ability to manage the politics, promote their own successes, and watch their own backs."
~ Simon Sinek

13

5

BECOMING AN EMPLOYER OF CHOICE

PEOPLE WHO WORK THERE
WANT TO KEEP WORKING THERE

*"At Chick-fil-A®, leaders **SERVE**, which means they do five things: **S**ee and shape the future; **E**ngage and develop others; **R**einvent continuously; **V**alue results and relationships; **E**mbody the company values."*
~ Dee Ann Turner, Chick-fil-A® VP Talent (Ret.)

To ensure our cultural vision remains aligned at this critical stage, let me clarify. Becoming an employer of choice means: The people who are currently working in your organization have a very strong desire to continue working there because they're excited about their future within the organization, there are frequent growth and development opportunities, they are consistently challenged to get better in positive ways, they feel valued by their leaders and their team, they have meaningful relationships with their co-workers, they feel good while on the job, and equally as important, they feel good about themselves and their leaders at the end of each day.

As I mentioned, the cultural transformation mountain is tall, steep, and challenging at times. If you're serious about developing a high impact culture, you may likely feel challenged. If you don't feel challenged by my last paragraph, you're either already there and trying to get better, or you have no real intentions of going there.

I assume you're reading this because you already know

you want to climb the mountain, or you're curious about climbing the mountain. Either way, don't let the challenge you may be feeling at this moment overwhelm you. You won't have to learn to climb alone. I'm here with you, and my mission is to help others climb.

My intention in the first six chapters is to help you understand why you should consider climbing the cultural transformation mountain. The remaining 24 chapters are intended to help you understand what you must do in order to climb the mountain. Not only will I describe what must be done, I'll also provide resources to aid you and your team as you begin your climb and offer a few key examples of how to climb.

Keep reading, thinking, reflecting, and making notes as you continue. Consider this book a guide, a road map, as I take you on a mental climb up the mountain before you strap your boots on and do it within your organization.

This book is intended to be a tool for high impact leaders who want to build a high performance team capable of creating a high impact culture. Jim Blanchard made a great point when he said, "When current or would-be leaders realize you are investing in their growth, it's more important to them than money."

To become highly effective at competing with those who want to steal your people, you must become an employer of choice. Otherwise, you'll find yourself on the losing end of the labor war, especially relative to attracting great people. The result: endless frustration.

Read the opening paragraph of this chapter again. Imagine the type of word of mouth advertisement someone with those feelings working at an employer of choice will provide. It will be off the charts. That type of word of mouth advertisement will cause any organization to become a sought after employer.

But, you can't buy that kind of advertisement. You must earn it. Here's an example of the impact.

Chick-fil-A® was our client for three years straight and is a great example of a sought after employer of choice. They've been climbing the mountain for over 50 years. They understand they don't have to be sick to get better and are striving relentlessly to improve.

I remember one store owner in a town of 30,000 saying to me, "When I have an entry-level job opening, I typically have 250 applicants." Wow! Without a doubt, there are always great people applying. That's what it means to be a sought after employer of choice.

To become a sought after blue-collar employer of choice, you must become innovative. Culture is all about the people, not your products and services. So, when I say innovative, I mean innovative relative to the growth and development of all people at all levels.

Why is growth and development of people innovative? It's not in the white-collar world, because they've been doing it for decades. But, it is in the blue-collar world because very few blue-collar leaders value doing it, even if they're considered successful within their industry.

Ria and I had the privilege of speaking at Yale University's School of Management on "Blue-Collar Leadership®: Innovation in Talent Development." You can watch the entire one hour video of our session on our home page at BlueCollarLeadership.com

"It can be far more difficult to overcome success than adversity...There's a tendency for many in successful companies to rest on their laurels and become complacent, self-protective, and less innovative. In such bureaucratic cultures, employees can survive only by running with the herd. Decline sets in."
~ Charles G. Koch, CEO Koch Industries

6

THE TRANSFORMATION EQUATION

DISCOVER THE 5 KEY COMPONENTS FOR BUILDING HIGH PERFORMANCE TEAMS

"Change starts with 'what is' and attempts to keep what is working intact and eliminate what is not, transformation simply starts with 'nothing' and is led by a vision of the whole as if it were to be created from scratch today. The former views today as an extension of yesterday and tries to make the most of what is. The latter sees today as the beginning of tomorrow and shapes today's circumstances as a solid foundation for what will be." ~ Amir Ghannad

I want to establish the foundation for the remainder of the book by introducing you to The Transformation Equation. Please turn to the end of this chapter to view an illustration. It's also contained in our Blue-Collar Leadership whitepaper which can be viewed at: GetTheTransformationEquation.com

The Transformation Equation reveals the components of transformation and the outcome when each is missing.

In the unfortunate event all components are missing, the outcome will be chaos. I've seen it, and I've worked in it. There's a good chance you have too. Unfortunately in many organizations, chaos is the norm not the exception.

Leadership Development comes first in the equation because it is absolutely the most important component.

LEADERSHIP DEVELOPMENT, or the lack of it, determines the leader's ability to transform the culture.

As you can see, Leadership Development is the key...

- to generating BUY-IN...without BUY-IN, there will be RESISTANCE
- to effectively casting the vision and defining the team's mission or UNIFYING PURPOSE... without a UNIFYING PURPOSE, there will be CONFUSION
- to developing their team's COMPETENCY relative to doing the job effectively and working well with others...without COMPETENCY, there will be ANXIETY
- to motivating and inspiring their team to move from planning to EXECUTION...without execution, there will be STAGNATION

Without LEADERSHIP DEVELOPMENT, there will be FRUSTRATION. I'll begin to help you better understand what I mean in the next chapter.

What I've shared with you above is self-evident. You can easily validate the outcome when a specific component is missing. All of the outcomes above result in negative word of mouth advertisement, not positive. Negative word of mouth advertisement makes it hard to find good people. It must be minimized or eliminated.

Therefore as the leader, it's your responsibility to prevent these outcomes.

Throughout the remaining chapters, I'll be providing many additional details and valuable insights about each of the components to help you better understand them and how to leverage them as you build a high performance team and create a high impact culture.

I speak to top leaders of blue-collar organizations and blue-collar business owners at various types of associations and conferences all across the USA. I've discovered those who haven't been focused on growing and developing the people within their organizations in the past have no idea what is involved or how to get started. Many of them are curious but don't really know why they should do it, if they really should do it, or if they can do it. Without competency, there's anxiety.

This book is for the leaders who want to answer those questions and many more. I've mentioned I intend it to be a tool, a manual, and a road map. Therefore, as I begin to share "how to do" and "what to do," you'll find book titles or links at the end of some chapters. You can reference them as team development resources. You can learn more about our other books in the back of this one.

Many leaders have never developed themselves relative to the principles I'm sharing. Therefore, they don't know what they don't know. But, many have a desire to learn.

If you're new to this type of content, please understand this book is intended only as an introduction to the type of leadership development that creates high impact cultures and builds high performance teams. I'll only skim the surface relative to leadership principles. I have many other books where leadership is the focus.

We could read everyday for 40 years and never learn it all. We should choose to become lifetime leadership students who are focused on inspiring others to do the same. Those who know the most about leadership are also those who know they'll never learn it all, no matter how long they live or how many books they read.

"The first step to creating a compelling culture for your team is to be assured of your calling as their leader."
~ Dee Ann Turner, Chick-fil-A® VP Talent (Ret.)

The Transformation Equation

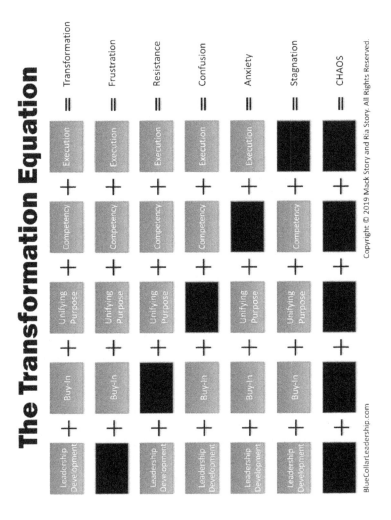

Leadership Development	+ Buy-In	+ Unifying Purpose	+ Competency	+ Execution	= Transformation
	+ Buy-In	+ Unifying Purpose	+ Competency	+ Execution	= Frustration
Leadership Development	+	+ Unifying Purpose	+ Competency	+ Execution	= Resistance
Leadership Development	+ Buy-In	+	+ Competency	+ Execution	= Confusion
Leadership Development	+ Buy-In	+ Unifying Purpose	+	+ Execution	= Anxiety
Leadership Development	+ Buy-In	+ Unifying Purpose	+ Competency	+	= Stagnation
	+	+	+	+	= CHAOS

COMPONENT 1
LEADERSHIP
DEVELOPMENT

7

MINIMIZE FRUSTRATION

WITHOUT LEADERSHIP DEVELOPMENT, THERE WILL BE FRUSTRATION

"Failing organizations are usually over-managed and under-led." ~ Warren Bennis

In failing or struggling organizations, there's always a lot of people at all levels who are experiencing frustration. Often, on a daily and maybe even an hourly basis. Frustration seems to never end. In many organizations, frustration is the norm, not the exception. Even in highly successful, well-led organizations, there will be frustration. However, there will be much less.

Merriam-Webster defines frustration as, "a deep chronic sense or state of insecurity and dissatisfaction arising from unresolved problems or unfulfilled needs."

Answer this simple question: The last time you were frustrated with a member, or members of your team, was it because you had too much influence or too little influence?

This question is intended to be thought-provoking. Pause and think deeply about it for a moment before you continue. Then, reflect on several more recent examples from your life, at work and away from work.

When we're frustrated, it's absolutely because we didn't have enough influence. Not sometime, every time. It's a fact at home and at work. It's true with team members, customers, suppliers, family members, and strangers. It's a principle: When we're frustrated, it's due to a lack of influence.

This principle is easily validated.

When my son was a teenager, I was often frustrated because I couldn't get him to do what I wanted him to do. In other words, I didn't have enough influence.

When I couldn't get someone on my team at work to buy-in to my idea, I was frustrated. Whether they reported to me, I reported to them, or we were peers on the same level. I simply didn't have enough influence.

Frustration occurs when we want something to happen, but it doesn't. Or, when we wanted to prevent something from happening, but we couldn't.

The root cause of both of my examples was my lack of influence. The root cause of the examples you thought about was your lack of influence. Ultimately, I was frustrated with myself and my inability to influence my desired outcome. It's the same for you too, whether you know it or not and whether you want to admit it or not.

To understand why leadership development is crucial to eliminating frustration, we must consider the definition of leadership.

Leadership is influence. Nothing more. Nothing less.

I learned this from John C. Maxwell. When I first read his definition, it was very thought-provoking.

I validated it quickly after asking myself, "Is the person with the most influence at any given time for any given reason in any given situation the leader?" Absolutely. Every time. The person with the most influence is the one determining the outcome at that moment in that situation. That person is leading, not following. They're not frustrated, although everyone else may be.

Leadership is not about position, title, and rank as

many believe. It's about influence. Do people with position, title, and rank have influence? Absolutely. But, not all the time and not with everyone. When they have influence, they are leading. When they don't have it, they are not leading and are likely frustrated as a result.

Therefore when there is frustration, it's due to a lack of leadership or influence. These words have the same meaning. The principles in this book and all of our other books will help you increase your influence and reduce your frustrations. Not when you read them, but when you learn to apply them and inspire others on your team to do the same.

Simon Sinek observed, "One of the great things that is lacking in most of our companies is that they are not teaching us how to lead. Managers must go through a transition—from being responsible for the job, to being responsible for the people who are responsible for the job." There's a big difference between doing a great job and being able to influence others to do a great job.

Leaders who are frustrated should consider Henry Cloud's words, "One of the biggest differences between successful people and others is that in love and in life, in relationships and in business, successful people always ask themselves…What part am I playing in this situation?"

Help your team discover the fundamentals of leadership and influence!
Visit: BlueCollarLeadership.com/Defining-Influence

"When we are in the presence of good leadership, we usually are not even aware of it. Everything goes so well that leadership seems unnecessary; it creates the illusion that everything is seamless and smooth."
~ Jimmy Collins, Chick-fil-A® President/COO (Ret.)

8

LEADING, FOLLOWING, AND MANAGING

EVERYONE IS A LEADER; EVERYONE IS A FOLLOWER; EVERYONE IS A MANAGER

"I believe ability can get you to the top, but it takes character to keep you there." ~ John Wooden

Leadership is influence. Influence can be positive or negative. Everyone has influence. However, the amount of influence each person has varies greatly. A person may have a lot of influence in one area and no influence in another area or with one person and not another.

Everyone influences others at some level. Therefore, everyone is a leader. Leaders have followers.

Everyone is being influenced by others. Therefore, everyone is also a follower. Followers choose leaders.

Everyone must also manage things and processes at some level. Therefore, everyone is a manager.

Regardless of our title, position, or rank, we are all leaders, followers, and managers. This includes those on the front lines in entry-level positions and everyone else.

Each person's overall level of effectiveness will be determined by their ability to be in the right role at the right time for the right reason in the right way. The collective effectiveness of the entire team will determine the effectiveness of the organization.

A person's character will determine how well they lead, how well they follow, and how well they manage. Leadership development equals character development.

The greater our character, the greater our positive influence. High performance teams always have high impact leaders who help each of them learn how to lead well, how to follow well, and how to manage well.

Low impact leaders do things much differently. They do a lot of hoping and wishing and very little, if any, developing. Hope is not a strategy, and wishful thinking doesn't improve teams.

Everyone has the capacity to increase their leadership ability. However, not everyone has a desire to do it. Some are happy to primarily follow. Others, who are in formal leadership positions, prefer to manage people instead of leading people. These managers are all great at the same thing: creating toxic cultures.

My friend and mentor, Jimmy Collins, Chick-fil-A® President/COO (Ret.), had this to say about leaders and followers, "A leader is someone who has followers. If there are no followers, there is no leader. A person may have subordinates, workers, admirers, associates, co-workers, friends, and people who report to him or her, a person may have authority over other people, a person may hold an elective office, and a person may influence a large number of people, but that does not make that person a leader if there are no followers. A follower is someone that has chosen a leader."

Many people believe organizational charts reveal who all of the leaders are in an organization. When you truly understand leadership, you'll know that's simply not true. An organizational chart reveals who all of the managers are because it's a management chart, not a leadership chart. These people are responsible for managing things and processes. Unfortunately, many of them choose to manage people too. They're still leaders, but they're low impact leaders. They won't be the ones who help you become a sought after employer of choice unless they make dramatic changes to their values and their character.

If you actually want to know who all of the leaders are in an organization, you'll simply need a list of all the employee's names. Each person on the list is a leader. Each of them is influencing the culture in a positive or negative way. Unfortunately, most aren't being developed.

Becoming a sought after employer of choice, will not happen without a tremendous amount of positive influence from your entire team, top to bottom. It will also require influence from those outside your organization. Your team must be capable of influencing others to talk positively about the organization too.

If the people on the inside speak positively about the organization, but the people on the outside speak negatively about the organization, prepare for frustration. You can't fake a high impact culture. You either have one or you don't. Leadership development is the foundation because you must use your entire workforce to generate as much authentic, positive influence as possible.

Your team's ability to serve your customers well and create positive word of mouth advertisement will be based on their ability to lead themselves and others well, follow others well, and manage things and processes well.

Help your team learn to effectively communicate in each of these roles!
Visit: RiaStory.com/Communication

"The strength of the culture, and not its size or resources, determines an organization's ability to adapt to the times, overcome adversity, and pioneer new innovations." ~ Simon Sinek

9

LEADERSHIP DEVELOPMENT NEVER ENDS

THE LANGUAGE OF LEADERSHIP IS EXTREMELY DYNAMIC AND COMPLEX

"Leadership.
It's one of the most misunderstood words in the
professional world, and perhaps in the
personal development world." ~ Ria Story

Once you get past the simple definition, "Leadership is influence," things start to get complicated and complex. Not because leadership principles are hard to understand but because of the endless number of variables that impact how our attempts at influence are perceived and received.

What one person perceives as positive may be perceived as negative by another person at the very same moment. When you're building trust with one person, you could be creating distrust with another. This is because different people have different values.

For example, I've walked into a room full of blue-collar supervisors and started talking about character development. Some were glad I was there, while others started rolling their eyes, snickering, and wondering why I was there.

Those who were glad I was there felt motivated because we had shared values. Those rolling their eyes felt manipulated because we didn't have shared values. Because of the difference in their values relative to mine, they saw me differently. I instantly began building trust with those with shared values. I instantly began creating distrust with those without shared values.

Trust is the foundation of leadership and is based on two components: character and competency. Research reveals that 87% of our influence is based on character and only 13% on competency. Without trust, there will be no authentic influence.

Intention is the foundation of trust. Intention is about motivation and manipulation. If someone believes there is mutual benefit, they feel motivated and trust is built. If they feel they are not benefiting, they feel manipulated and distrust is created. Just as we decide how others make us feel, they decide how we make them feel. This is where influence gets even more complex.

Every interaction with every person is different every time. Why? Things are constantly changing at work, at home, and in the world. To complicate relationships, each person has different beliefs, different values, different experiences, different expectations, different goals, different motives, different personalities, different things going on in their lives, different competencies, different fears, different dreams, different strengths, different weaknesses, different character, and on and on.

Each of us is extremely unique, but very similar.

After reading and studying about leadership literally every day since 2008, I know I will always be a student.

Leadership development for me will never end.

We must manage things and processes because they don't think and feel, but we should lead people because they do. If you choose to begin a leadership development initiative, what you'll be attempting to do is align everyone behind a set of unifying leadership principles.

If you don't, everyone will be going in multiple directions for multiple reasons and exhibiting behavior based on the values they brought to work with them. The result will be chaos fueled by frustrations based on distrust, lack of communication, finger-pointing, ruptured relationships, short-tempers, pride, ego, and low morale.

Aligning everyone behind proven, unifying leadership principles is the key to avoiding chaos and creating a high impact culture. The difference between a principle and a practice is that a principle applies in all situations with all people, at all times. But, a practice only applies in certain situations, with certain people, at certain times.

I compare understanding leadership to understanding the English language.

If you learn the 26 letters of the alphabet, how much do you know about the English language? Not much. You must learn to combine letters to form words. Then, you must learn to combine words into sentences. Then, you discover there's hidden meanings between the words. Then, you discover one word can have many meanings depending on "how" it's spoken. Learning leadership is very similar, but much more dynamic.

Discover 30 key characteristics of very successful leaders!
Visit: RiaStory.com/LeadershipGems

"Our capacity for development does not end at physical maturity; our capacity is virtually limitless. Our power to reason is our distinguishing characteristic, our mind is our basic means of survival—and our ability to think, to learn, to discover new and better ways of dealing with reality, to expand the range of our efficacy, to grow intellectually, is an open door to a road that has no end." ~ Ayn Rand

10

THE LEADERSHIP DILEMMA

YOU CAN'T DEVELOP OTHERS
WITHOUT DEVELOPING YOURSELF

*"Becoming a leader is a lifelong endeavor of
study, action, reflection, and refinement."*
~ Colonel Tom Connally, USMC (Ret.)

When you consider the Leadership Development component in The Transformation Equation, you should know it consists of two parts: development of self and development of others. Developing others is not about you, but it starts with you.

As a leader with a desire to create a high impact culture that will ensure your organization becomes a highly sought after employer of choice, your primary role is to lead the charge up the mountain. Since you're not literally climbing a mountain, this means you must be the model of what you expect from others because someone is always watching, especially during culture change.

My favorite quote of all time is by Abraham Maslow, "If we are not modeling what we're teaching, we are teaching something else." What Maslow means is you're not teaching what you're teaching. You're teaching what you're modeling. Actions truly do speak louder than words.

High impact leadership is more caught than taught.

Do you want your team to see you as a tour guide or a travel agent? There's a big difference.

Often, travel agents have never been to the places they're telling others they should go. They tell them how wonderful the "climb up the mountain" will be and what they will experience along the way. But, they've never actually made the climb themselves.

However, a tour guide has "been up the mountain" many times. Their mission is to lead others up the mountain, not direct them over the radio from base camp (or the front office).

Who would you trust most? The travel agent who has never made the climb and has no interest in joining you, or the tour guide who has made the journey many times and wants to lead you? Which will your team see?

Some reading this may be thinking, "Well, I'm neither at the moment. I've never directed a cultural transformation or led a team through one." If that's the case with you, consider me a guide willing to help you and your team climb. But, here's the question you must answer: As my team's leader, will I be applying for the job of travel agent or tour guide?

An organization with a leader who attempts to create a high impact culture as a travel agent will never become a sought after employer of choice as I describe. Why? Because those on their team who actually follow the directions of their "travel agent" leader will outgrow their leader who isn't on the journey with them.

When this happens, these team members will become frustrated because of their leader's lack of leadership development. They will come to understand their leader is disengaged, so they will disengage. They will either give bad word of mouth advertisement about the leader and the organization, or they will leave the company in search of a better leader. Most often, they will do both.

You're reading this book which means you're already

developing yourself. However, to create the culture I've described in the previous chapters, you must become very intentional about your own personal development. Don't stop doing what you're doing now. Although it helps to be at the top of the class, and I think you should be, the main thing is that your team sees you in class and knows you're on the development journey with them.

The additional book titles and links at the end of related chapters are to help accelerate your climb. Reading books is one way to grow, but it's not the only way.

You can also listen to podcasts or audiobooks. You can watch videos. I have more than 130 short (3 to 8 minute) videos based on many of my books for you and your team to learn from at YouTube.com/c/mackstory

If the team isn't performing, it's because the leader isn't serving. Consider this as you read the closing quote by Bob Chapman. He leads a $3 billion global supplier of manufacturing technology and solutions with over 12,000 employees. Bob is a high impact leader serving a high performance team that serves their customers well.

Help leaders align themselves with key leadership values in Mack's book:
10 Values of High Impact Leaders

Listen to our podcasts and samples of our audiobooks at:
TopStoryLeadership.com/podcast
TopStoryLeadership.com/audiobooks

"We make some of the best industrial machinery in the world. But, I will not go to my grave being proud of all the machines we have built. Instead, I will be deeply grateful for all the lives that we touched and uplifted in our journey. The machinery we build is just the economic engine that enables us to touch lives. The flourishing of those lives is our paramount concern."
~ Bob Chapman, CEO Barry-Wehmiller

11

DEVELOP HIGH IMPACT INDIVIDUALS

PERSONAL DEVELOPMENT
IS THE FOUNDATION OF
LEADERSHIP DEVELOPMENT

"We understand that talented people with bad values can do far more damage to a company than virtuous people with inferior talents."
~ Charles G. Koch, CEO Koch Industries

You can't transform the culture of your organization by yourself, but you must begin the cultural transformation within yourself.

Cultural transformation cannot happen without individual transformation. Each individual on your team must choose to change their values just as you must choose to change your own. I can't make you. I can only influence you. You can't make them. You can only influence them.

Regardless of how many times you've heard, "There's no 'I' in Team," you must understand there are multiple "I's" on every team. If your team is made up of 10 people, there are 10 "I"ndividuals on your team. If your team is made up of 10,000 people, there are 10,000 "I"ndividuals on your team. Each team member is an "I" and will always be an "I." A team is simply a group of "I"ndividuals.

Without high impact "I"ndividuals, there won't be a high performance team. As John C. Maxwell said, "When you equip people, you teach them how to do a job. When you develop them, you are helping them to improve as individuals." Cultural transformation is about developing and improving "I"ndividuals.

I'll introduce you to a resource in this chapter that will help you develop high impact "I"ndividuals at every level. You should start your formal cultural transformation at the "I"ndividual level, and one of the best ways to do that is with books. Start conducting book studies with your team to begin unleashing their potential.

Select books with content everyone needs to align themselves with such as character development, building trust, teamwork, etc. There are thousands of books available. Next, develop and execute a plan to methodically introduce them to everyone at every level. How often you do it, how deep you go into the material, and how long it will take to cover a book will vary based on the book size and organization size. Then, select books for certain support teams or various levels of leadership such as relationship selling books for your sales team, leader focused books for your formal authority leaders, and books on leading teams for those who may be leading process improvement teams. To get some help, visit BlueCollarLeadership.com/implement.

I encourage you, and anyone with a desire, to read as many books as possible, but you should also slow down and be methodical when it comes to effectively implementing your leadership development program throughout your organization.

My book, Blue-Collar Leadership®: Leading from the Front Lines, is a resource for leaders who want to start developing "I"ndividuals, especially those "I"ndividuals on the front lines in entry-level, blue-collar positions. It's full of principles that will improve the character of each

"I"ndividual on your team, regardless of their position, title, rank, job, department, or age. Your goal should always be to get everyone on your team aligned with the same fundamental character-based principles.

As the leader of the cultural transformation, you must also read it and ensure you're learning and modeling the principles for your entire team. Once you introduce them to it and expect them to embrace it, they'll look to see if you and other leaders are also attempting to embrace and understand it.

From 1988-2008, I worked in the manufacturing industry. The first 10 years, I was an entry-level machine operator on the front lines. The second 10 years I was in support roles such as engineering, process improvement, and management. During those 20 years, there wasn't a single leader who introduced me or my co-workers to the type of content you'll find in my books.

I wrote Blue-Collar Leadership® as the book I wish a leader would have shared with me during those first 10 years on the front lines. It would have changed my life and accelerated my career. Use it to help your team be better and live better. When you do, they'll respect you, follow you, and speak positively about you.

Ria and I recently spoke to nearly 150 employees at a blue-collar organization where the owner had introduced it to his entire team. In just a few months, productivity and morale were up, and absenteeism was down.

Help all of your team members learn how to lead themselves well!
Visit: BlueCollarLeadership.com/Workers

"If enough people declare themselves, individually, the cause of the current culture, and unconditionally commit to a different behavior, we can shift the culture instantly." ~ Amir Ghannad

12

DEVELOP HIGH IMPACT
TEAM PLAYERS

HELP TEAM MEMBERS LEARN "HOW TO BE" WHILE THEY'RE DOING WHAT THEY DO

*"Leadership is an ability and responsibility for all.
Our definition of leadership is the ability to make
those around you better and more productive."*
~ Jack Clark

When you develop high impact individuals, you're building the foundation upon which high impact team players can be developed. First you help your team members learn to lead themselves well. Then, you help them learn how to intentionally work effectively with others.

As Peyton Manning remarked, "The most valuable player is the one that makes the most players valuable."

Your goal as you lead culture transformation should be to become this type of MVP. When you're creating a high impact culture, your goal is to make as many of your team members as valuable to the organization as possible. It's about far more than getting them to do their job and perform their tasks. You should see each of them as a brand ambassador for your organization. When you do, you'll want to develop them continuously and relentlessly.

We're often asked, "Do you do any type of training and development specifically for teams?" I always reply,

"If you're referring to interactive team-based activities that forces people to work together in an effort to build better relationships, such as rope courses, obstacle courses, games, team challenges, etc., the answer is no. We do not do that. However, everything we do is about team building."

Consider this example. Assume you assemble a team of 10 strangers. Each of them has the competency to do their job, and each has well-developed character: trustworthy, willing to listen to the opinions of others, takes responsibility, gives credit to others when things go right, accepts the blame when things go wrong, controls their emotions, helps others succeed, shows up on time with a great attitude, and likes working with others.

Imagine this team of strangers. Do you think they would need team-based training before they could work effectively together as a team? Absolutely not, they would hit the ground running and never stop.

Now consider this example. Assume you assemble a team of 10 people who have worked together for years. Each of them has the competency to do their job, but each has poor character: untrustworthy, unwilling to listen to the opinions of others, avoids responsibility, takes credit when things go right, blames others when things go wrong, can't control their emotions, focused on their own success, shows up late with a bad attitude, and prefers to work alone.

Imagine this team of co-workers. Do you think completing a rope course with their co-workers is going to change their character? Absolutely not. Their relationships may improve a bit because they get to know each other without the job-related stress. But, who they are at the core, their character, will remain unchanged. Character is developed daily, not in a day.

When it comes to building high impact team players, dramatically different values always lead to dramatically different results. The difference between a high impact player and a low impact player is their values. Values determine how they think and what they do.

My book, Blue-Collar Leadership® & Teamwork: 30 Traits of High Impact Players, is a resource that will help leaders develop high impact team players. High impact players don't just do things different. Because their character is different, they are different.

I recommend introducing all team members to Blue-Collar Leadership® first to establish a solid foundation. Then, introduce Blue-Collar Leadership® & Teamwork to help take each team member to the next level and beyond.

Blue-Collar Leadership® & Teamwork has 30 chapters with titles like: Be Responsible, Be Trustworthy, Be Positive, Be Flexible, Be Open-Minded, Be Helpful, and Be Approachable.

Leadership development at all levels is not something you do once or every now and then. It must become part of the culture. There must be a constant drip. High impact cultures require a lot of fuel because the people are hungry for growth. If you don't feed those great people who are hungry for growth, someone else will.

High impact players require high impact leaders.

Help your team learn "how to be" while they're doing what they do!
Visit: BlueCollarLeadership.com/Teamwork

"When we look at people who disobey their leaders, the first question we ought to ask is not, 'What's wrong with those people?' but rather, 'What's wrong with their leader?' It says that responsibility begins at the top." ~ Malcolm Gladwell

13

DEVELOP HIGH IMPACT LEADERS

THE LEVEL OF ENGAGEMENT BELOW IS DETERMINED BY THE LEVEL OF ENGAGEMENT ABOVE

"Often, organizations focus only on the value of developing new leaders and neglect the development of seasoned leaders. A few will take their thinking to the next level and continue to invest in seasoned leaders. Organizations that invest in both new leadership and seasoned leaders will clearly create the most competitive workforce."
~ Dee Ann Turner, Chick-fil-A® VP Talent (Ret.)

As you develop individuals and help them become high impact team players, you're actually beginning to fill your leadership pipeline. That's why I say personal development is the foundation for leadership development. You shouldn't expect someone to be able to lead others well until they've proven they can lead themselves well. However, in many organizations, there's little, if any, focus on leadership development at any level.

Most often in blue-collar industries, someone who demonstrates their ability to do a job well is the one promoted into a leadership position. Then, the vast majority of them struggle at leading others well. Most can manage their team, but few can lead their team.

Often, the people who have the courage to step up when asked end up being bashed and blamed by their boss when they struggle. A boss who likely hasn't had any leadership development. The lack of leadership development above always leads to frustrations below.

The best leaders were always the best followers first. The two books I recommended as resources in the previous two chapters will help team members at every level learn how to follow well as they learn how get exceptional results by leading themselves well. Those who are the best at leading themselves well will also be best at modeling and teaching others to do the same.

You will no longer have to search for good people because you'll be developing great people. Your challenge will not be finding the next person on your team to promote when a leadership position needs to be filled. It will be deciding who deserves it most.

High performance teams have leader-follower relationships instead of boss-worker relationships.

Jimmy Collins, Chick-fil-A® President/COO (Ret.) had this to say about the boss-worker relationship, "We must clearly understand the difference between the role of a worker and the role of a follower. A worker is someone who does a job. A worker is not a follower, although a worker could potentially become a follower. A worker works for a boss. A boss is the person with positional authority over workers. Being a boss has nothing to do with how well or how poorly a person does his or her job. All the word boss signifies is the person who oversees the activities of the workers."

The boss-worker relationship is the most common throughout blue-collar industries. In Jimmy's example, I refer to the boss as a manager of people. There is no leadership. There is only snoopervision and directing.

Bosses don't take responsibility for how well their workers are performing. Instead, they blame them.

Workers work for a boss because they feel they have to. Followers work with a leader because they want to. Research has shown that followers are 40% more productive on average than workers.

High impact individuals on your front line, who have been developed and are leading themselves well, expect and deserve to be led well. It's your responsibility to ensure they have leaders worth following. The #1 reason people quit is the relationship with their boss. Leaders are responsible for turnover and retention.

My book, Blue-Collar Leadership® & Supervision: Unleash Your Team's Potential, is a foundational resource for you to use as you begin developing your formal authority leaders. It serves as an introduction to high impact leadership and will help them attract more followers, improve morale, gain buy-in, and maximize productivity. All formal leaders at every level need to learn and apply the principles they'll discover in it. It's the starting point, but only after they've been introduced to the previous two books I've recommended.

You should also introduce it to those in entry-level positions who show potential as you begin to prepare them for their first formal leadership role. Invite them to development sessions with the formal leaders.

Help every leader at every level learn how to lead others well!
Visit: BlueCollarLeadership.com/Leaders

"Whether in the military or a civilian organization, the culture of the first organization a young person joins has tremendous impact. And, his or her first immediate supervisor significantly shapes that person's understanding of the organization and the role of supervisors and managers."
~ Colonel Tom Connally, USMC (Ret.)

14

BECOMING A
TRANSFORMATIONAL LEADER

LEADERS ARE ALWAYS TEACHING WHAT
THEY'RE MODELING, REGARDLESS
OF WHAT THEY'RE TEACHING

*"Creating a beneficial culture is impossible
without mentoring and positive examples."*
~ Charles G. Koch, CEO Koch Industries

Ria and I recently conducted a multi-day workshop on Transformational Leadership for the Association for Talent Development in Washington D. C. The following is an excerpt from material Ria created for that event:

The need for culture transformation can be driven by one or more key factors: organizational growth, toxic organizational culture, poor top-level leadership, industry or technology changes, negativity, poor management, or even a lack of succession planning for an aging workforce. Anytime we are trying to create positive change, we find ourselves challenged to influence others to accept, buy-in, and get on board with, the change and transformation. In an uncertain world, one thing is certain: leading positive transformation is challenging.

Transformation is a change in form, appearance, or character. Transformational Leaders influence others to change their character, and therefore their behavior.

Few people have a desire to truly become a

down to find others who need help climbing to the top.
Transformational Leaders sacrifice personally in order to
become significant in the lives of others. The challenges
will be great, and the obstacles will be endless.

However, the reward is priceless. Transformational
Leadership is about making a difference in the lives of
others. It's about fulfilling your purpose and helping
someone else unleash their potential. Transformational
Leadership is about refusing to accept good enough and
go for great. As Jim Collins, author of Good to Great
said, "Good is the enemy of great. And, that is one of the
key reasons why we have so little that becomes great."

Regardless of whether you're an Owner, CEO,
Director, HR Professional, Consultant, Trainer, or Talent
Development Specialist, you have the opportunity to
move beyond simply managing the tasks of your daily job.
You have the opportunity to move from good to great,
personally and professionally, when you accept the
responsibility of becoming a Transformational Leader.

There are two requirements: personal transformation
and a high level of positive influence.

You must have undergone transformation yourself
before you can lead others through it. You cannot give
someone something you don't have to give. You can't
take them to the top of the mountain if you don't know
the way.

You must be able to influence others, relative to

44

improving their character by changing their values, in a transformational and positive way. Influence is the essence of leadership and positive influence is the key to transformational leadership because we are asking someone to follow us somewhere they have never been. Quite possibly, they don't believe in themselves as much as we believe in their potential. We must be able to motivate them to change and to sustain that motivation until they become inspired enough to continue the journey without as much, or any, support. If it sounds hard and time consuming, that's because it is.

In truth, we cannot force someone to change their values. But, we can influence them. OUR ability to coach and develop others not just in the job competencies, but also on the personal character side, determines if we will become more than just a competent "manager" of the job itself but also a "Transformational Leader" of others. Someone who, regardless of formal level of authority, can take an organization from "good to great."

Discover the 10 Foundational Elements of Intentional Transformation!
Visit: BlueCollarLeadership.com/Transformation

"We all know, whether we actually practice it or not, that basic respect and courtesy should not depend on the person's title or rank. What we forget sometimes is that it should also not depend on a person's performance. It is possible to share tough feedback and hold low performers to high standards without treating them as lesser human beings. Transformative Leaders have the courage to create a culture of accountability AND the consideration to treat everyone with dignity and respect, all the way through the performance correction process."
~ Amir Ghannad

COMPONENT 2
BUY-IN

15

ELIMINATE RESISTANCE

WITHOUT BUY-IN,
THERE WILL BE RESISTANCE

*"People buy into the leader first,
then the leader's vision." ~ John C. Maxwell*

In The Transformation Equation, Leadership Development comes before Buy-In because of the principle contained in Maxwell's quote above. Leadership Development is the key to generating Buy-In, especially when you're trying to get people to buy into cultural transformation because developing effective, positive influence is the only way to get them to move from where they are to where you want them to be.

When the team doesn't buy-in to the leader, there will always be resistance. The team will be frustrated and the leader will be frustrated. When people are resisting their leader's influence, they will be disengaged.

No one can be resistant and engaged at the same time. People resist specifically because they don't want to engage. They may be resistant while being paid to be at work, but that doesn't mean they have bought into the leader's mission and vision. They may be at work, but they won't be as productive as they could be.

Disengagement is simply a passive form of resistance.

I'm always amazed at the time, energy, and financial resources that are continuously spent on employee engagement surveys year after year as they continue to reveal that nothing is changing with the passing of time. 65-70% of employees on average continue to remain disengaged. In other words, they're not bought-in to their leaders. This statistic hasn't changed in the past 30 years or more. Leaders are still continuing to ask, "Why?"

For those who have a deep understanding of high impact leadership, the answer to "Why?" is very clear: The people aren't engaged because their leaders aren't engaged. The leaders may be extremely engaged when it comes to managing the people, but they're extremely disengaged when it comes to leading the people. Without effective leadership development, there will not be effective leadership of people.

Managers of people conduct employee engagement surveys because they don't know what they don't know about leadership. This doesn't mean they're bad people or dumb people. They simply can't know what they don't know. Conducting an engagement survey is a management activity. Another attempt at managing the people like objects.

Doing something about engaging the disengaged is a leadership activity. However, if those managers of people actually knew what to do about the survey results, they would already be doing it and wouldn't be spending time and money conducting a survey. If they were capable of leading the people to begin with, they wouldn't have a reason to conduct a survey because the people would already be bought-in and engaged.

As long as management of people continues, disengagement will continue. Nothing will change except the people due to high turnover and low retention.

Buying-in is about wanting to, not having to. If people had to buy-in, there would be 100% engagement instead of 30-35%. Without a transformational leader to lead the way, the disengaged will never become engaged because they don't have to, and they don't want to.

If you buy-in and act upon what I'm presenting to you in this book, that transformational leader will be you.

If you're resistant and not fully buying-in and think there's another way, an easier way, or that what I'm proposing will never really work, it will not be you.

There's only one way to create a high impact culture and to build a high performance team that will make your organization a sought after employer of choice within your industry and in your area of operation. It's the way I'm introducing in this book. However, I'm only scratching the surface of what will ultimately be required.

When I say there's only one way, I mean you must develop your character and the character of your team members. There is no other way.

Managers of people have insufficiently developed character and lack leadership ability. Therefore, they demand buy-in and struggle to get it. Leaders of people have well-developed character and leadership ability. They achieve significant buy-in because they seek to earn it and refuse to demand it.

Every character-based personal growth and leadership development book is full of principles that will help you build trust, generate buy-in, and engage your team.

Help your team learn personal foundational success principles!
Visit: RiaStory.com/Achieve

"Only organizations with a sterling level of trust garner a culture of true commitment vs. a whirlpool of wishful thinking through forced compliance."
~ Pete Beaudrault

16

GENERATE BUY-IN

THE KEY TO OVERCOMING RESISTANCE

"If you think you're too busy to give time and energy to your people, then they're too busy to give time and energy to you. It is a balanced equation."
~ Simon Sinek

How do you generate buy-in? It's simple really. You involve the people. No involvement, no commitment. If you want your team to be committed, involve them in a meaningful way.

How do you involve the people in a meaningful way? You communicate with them. I don't mean one-way communication that managers prefer. I mean two-way communication that leaders prefer.

High impact leaders know one of the most effective communication tools is a question. As Andrew Sobel stated, "Telling creates resistance. Asking creates relationships." Resistance leads to more disengagement. Relationships lead to more engagement.

Telling or giving directions is one-way communication. It's fast, but it's inefficient, especially when it comes to building a high impact culture. Why? Because resistant people don't move very fast, if at all. You can't just walk in and tell everyone what you want them to value and how you want them to behave going forward and expect it to happen.

Asking questions leads to two-way communication.

Two-way communication leads to connection. One-way communication is about sharing information. Many managers don't even do that well. They tend to withhold information from their team for many flawed reasons. Two-way communication is about more than information. It's about connection which leads to motivation, inspiration, and transformation.

The outdated methods of communication such as telling people what to do and "If I want your opinion, I'll give it to you," are used by those trying to control the people. Those management methods are totally ineffective if you're trying to release the people's potential in an effort to become a sought after employer of choice.

You and your formal leaders must get close to people if you want to truly motivate and inspire them to buy-in and help you take the organization to the next level and beyond. You're still reading this, so I assume you have some interest. My intent is to help you climb, not to help you remain the same.

What you already know is what got you and your team to where you are today. If things were supposed to be different, they would already be different. One thing I always told the hundreds of process improvement teams I led was, "If you want dramatically different results, you must do things dramatically different."

The people and the organization are always exactly where their leader has led them. How could they be anyplace else? They shouldn't be and couldn't be.

High impact leadership is about taking responsibility. If buy-in is low, it's because the leader's ability to lead is low. What can be done? Develop the leader or accept the resistance. You'll be responsible for developing the leaders and yourself if it's your direct team, or you'll be responsible for not developing the leaders and allowing or potentially causing the resistance. That's a hard pill for managers to swallow because their instinct leads them toward blame and away from responsibility.

For example, I remember walking into a hostile environment as a Lean Manufacturing consultant on a Monday to lead a group of people I had never met through a process improvement event. Our mission was to increase productivity on a new product line. The deadline to go live was near. Instead of accomplishing the mission, they were preparing to outsource some work. They were desperate, tired, and mad. Their leader was mad too because his leader brought me in to help.

They were a new client. It was my first time there. I had never worked in their industry. The general manager was on the team. He was cussing and badmouthing me in front of his team on day one. He had been blaming everyone and everything for his lack of success. Now, he was blaming me too and indirectly his boss.

I had five days to get results with a hostile team that knew nothing about me, Lean, or Leadership. The first thing I did was start two-way communication to build relationships and gain buy-in. I didn't start telling. I started asking. I was now responsible because I was the new leader. For me, blaming wasn't an option.

I provided Lean and Leadership training. Then, we got busy. The result: 376% productivity increase. It wasn't my fault the leader didn't know what he didn't know. He hadn't taken responsibility for learning lean or leadership.

Help your leaders learn to unleash process improvement teams like I did!
Visit: BlueCollarLeadership.com/Kaizen

*"A good route to executive failure is to be
a part-time role model."*
~ Jimmy Collins, Chick-fil-A® President/COO (Ret.)

17

LEADING CHANGE

WITHOUT CHANGE,
THERE CAN BE NO IMPROVEMENT

*"The great thing about business is that despite all
the history, all the deeply embedded traditional
dysfunctional management practices, and all the
baggage of unhealthy relationships and corrosive
cultures, it is possible at any moment in time to push
the reset button, to embrace a different way of
being, and experience dramatic change."*
~ Bob Chapman, CEO Barry-Wehmiller

Change happens, and it will always happen. Everything
is constantly changing. People are changing. Customers
are changing. Suppliers are changing. Products are
changing. Expectations are changing. Goals are changing.
Demand for products is changing. Equipment is
changing. Technology is changing.

I believe the greatest resistance is the resistance to
change. For this reason, to gain buy-in when change
happens, you must develop your team very intentionally
in this area. You must help them embrace a growth-
mindset because many people have a fixed-mindset.

In other words, you must help them see the positive
benefits change can bring to them and the organization.
High impact individuals with a growth-mindset leverage
change. They've discovered when change happens, low
impact individuals whine. So, they choose to shine.

Who has more positive influence with you when you must initiate, implement, or lead change? The whiners or the shiners? The answer is obvious. It's the shiners who aren't resisting the change. The shiners aren't just neutral. They're actually helping you make the changes and helping you gain buy-in from other team members while the whiners are moaning, groaning, and dragging others down. Is your team full of whiners or shiners?

High impact individuals with a growth-mindset go beyond embracing and supporting change. In fact, they initiate change and seek change. These are high value individuals. They're not happy maintaining the status quo. They're looking for and making process improvements without being asked or told.

Consider the example of the general manager in the story I shared at the end of the last chapter. I have hundreds of similar stories with the same dramatic results.

The general manager had been working for over 30 years, but he had a fixed-mindset. He only changed when he had to. He was a manager of people, and that's all he ever planned to be. He had never taken the initiative to learn the process improvement principles of Lean Manufacturing or the leadership principles related to influencing others effectively. And worst of all, he constantly blamed his team for being exactly where he had led them. He didn't have the ability or desire to lead them at a higher level and obviously couldn't teach them what he didn't know. He wasn't a bad guy. He was just a manager of activities and people, a boss with workers.

I'm constantly blown away by the large number of low impact formal authority leaders with fixed-mindsets who don't seek growth relative to their responsibilities. Organizations with engagement, turnover, and retention issues are full of them. These low impact leaders can be found resting on their position, title, authority, and success. Unfortunately, many are at the top blaming their teams for their many frustrations. They don't want to change, and no one can make them.

A high impact leader with a growth-mindset says to themselves, "People report to me. I need to become a better leader, so I can motivate and inspire my team to get better and be more productive. I'm responsible for processes, so I need to learn process improvement principles and techniques. Then, I need to teach them to my team and help them learn to apply them."

When it comes to cultural transformation, you can change without transforming, but you can't transform without changing. Change will be the only constant as you climb the cultural transformation mountain. You can't take a step without everything changing.

When we teach, we change what people know. When we transform, we change who people are and how they do what they do.

Bob Chapman, CEO Barry-Wehmiller, believes, "With sustained caring leadership and clearly articulated and deeply ingrained values, organizations can develop an 'immunity to negative change,' a dynamic in which only forward movement is possible."

Our book, Change Happens: Leading Yourself and Others through Change, is a resource for leaders who want to help their team members develop a growth-mindset. In it, we help you release your team's potential by taking the complex and making it simple.

Help your team learn to embrace, support, and buy-in to change!
Visit: BlueCollarLeadership.com/Leading-Change

"Don't settle for just 'Managing Change!' Take on 'Leading a Transformation!'" ~ Amir Ghannad

COMPONENT 3
UNIFYING
PURPOSE

18

REDUCE CONFUSION

WITHOUT A UNIFYING PURPOSE, THERE WILL BE CONFUSION

"It's not enough to have purpose yourself.
You have to create a sense of purpose for others."
~ Mark Zuckerberg

People will be resistant and less likely to buy-in if they're confused about what's happening and why it's happening. Not because they're bad people or have a desire to annoy their leaders, but simply because they want to understand. It's human nature to want to understand what's going on around you and why. No one enjoys feeling confused about anything at anytime.

This applies to all organizational activities, not just culture change. If you don't establish a unifying purpose, the rumor mill and the grapevine will do it for you. People will start guessing, wondering, and talking to others inside and outside the organization without really knowing what's going on. You can't stop it. That's what people do. This only adds to the confusion. It also wastes a lot of time and energy at all levels.

I'm sure you've been a dark room before and understand how confusing it can be without your vision. Without a unifying purpose, your team will be confused.

Within the organization, the unifying purpose provides vision. As a leader, your goal should be to build trust by keeping people out of "the dark." Keeping people in "the dark" creates distrust. Low impact, insecure leaders keep people in "the dark" intentionally because having a confused team gives them a sense of control. They know what's going on and their team doesn't. Low impact leaders actually like it that way. They feel the need to control the thoughts and actions of others.

These low impact leaders are having a negative impact on the organizational culture because they create confusion. They won't take the time and have no desire to cast the vision and establish a unifying purpose. They don't want to deal with all the questions and unsolicited suggestions their team would likely have. They simply want people to do what they're told. These leaders attempt to force buy-in and avoid earning it.

This low impact leader mindset will prevent the development of a high performance team and a high impact culture.

High impact, secure leaders want their teams to understand because they know the impact it will have on morale, buy-in, trust, and productivity. They also know if their team understands the purpose, the vision, and the mission, they can help ensure success, help avoid and identify obstacles, and hold each other accountable. High impact leaders invite questions and suggestions from their team. They know no one is as smart as everyone.

Many leaders make the mistake of failing to effectively establish the unifying purpose when they begin to intentionally transform their organization's culture. They often simply get started. The only person in the organization who really knows what's going on and why is the leader and potentially those who are involved in the training sessions or book studies.

In this book, relative to culture change, I'm attempting to establish the following unifying purpose: To become a sought after employer of choice. I added the "Culture" section at the start to communicate the unifying purpose. If you buy-in, you and I will become unified relative to the mission and vision.

Once we're unified and in agreement with the purpose, the vision, and the mission, you're more likely to want to hear what else I have to say. You're also more likely to continue buying-in as long as I can effectively show you how what I'm asking you to do supports the overall unifying purpose.

Although there's a "why to do" culture section at the front of this book, there still needs to be a supporting "why to do" section for each component. For example, this chapter is my "why to do" relative to influencing you to establish and communicate the unifying purpose on the front end for your team.

All supporting sections of this book related to the five components of The Transformation Equation include additional "why to do" content that is aligned with and supports the overall unifying purpose, but I've also started focusing on the "what to do" and will soon begin introducing some "how to do" content.

As a leader, you need to know who is with you and who is against you. When you establish the unifying purpose, you'll likely see a division within the organization as two groups begin to form. Those who are supportive and positive will move toward you. Those who are resistant and negative will move away from you.

"If you could get all the people in an organization rowing in the same direction, you could dominate any industry, in any market, against any competition, at any time." ~ Patrick Lencioni

19

CLARIFY THE UNIFYING PURPOSE

THE LEADER'S RESPONSIBILITY IS TO CAST THE VISION AND DETERMINE THE MISSION

*"Followers choose to follow a leader with a compelling
purpose, vision, cause, or goal, the unifying purpose.
It is the leader's unifying purpose that attracts the
interest and loyalty of followers. The leader is
someone who is able to communicate unifying
purpose in a manner that is inspiring, persuasive,
or motivating. The unifying purpose
joins the followers to the leader."*
~ *Jimmy Collins, Chick-fil-A® President/COO (Ret.)*

Beyond being a resource for you personally, this book has a second purpose. It can also be used by leaders to establish and clarify the unifying purpose relative to cultural transformation. I highly recommend introducing it to all formal authority leaders at every level, along with having a discussion related to "What is our culture and why does it matter?" The best way to introduce it and discuss it is through a book study led by you.

Otherwise, you'll be the only one with the vision of what needs to happen and why. The rest of your leadership team will be "in the dark." That's not where you want them to be.

As you undertake this journey, you'll need all the help you can get. You'll need to decrease resistance and confusion while generating buy-in. If you haven't done any leadership development with your team previously, I recommend having all formal authority leaders read and discuss this book before actual leadership development begins. This book does contain high level leadership principles, but it's meant to prepare leaders for the cultural journey that lies ahead as you attempt to raise awareness, cast the vision, and generate buy-in.

By introducing all of your formal leaders to this content before you cast the vision to everyone and attempt to generate buy-in across the entire organization, you're preparing and equipping your cultural transformation support team. When all formal leaders are aligned and aware of what you're doing and why you're doing it, they'll be prepared to help you cast the vision. When the questions start coming in from all directions as word about the change starts spreading, they can help you generate buy-in.

Stephen M. R. Covey remarked, "While our motives and agendas are deep inside in our own hearts and minds, they become visible to others through our behaviors and as we share them with others." As you cast the vision and define the mission, you'll eliminate confusion by helping others understand your motive and agenda.

However, if you and your leadership team don't align your behavior with the message you're spreading and the vision you're casting, you'll only be adding to the confusion. You'll become part of the problem instead of becoming part of the solution.

I've recommended in previous chapters to intentionally get everyone aligned by formally and methodically introducing the same development content to everyone at the same time. This sends the message, "We're all in this together; no one is exempt. We will all learn together and should hold each other accountable."

If you're not the top leader in the organization, you must try to leverage your influence and get this book into the hands of the top leader. If you're bought-in after reading it, invest the time preparing to introduce it to the top leader. This will be your time to lead up.

Anyone at anytime can absolutely impact and begin to improve the culture. However, what I'm describing in this book can only be achieved from the top down. The top leader must be bought-in, must cast the vision, must initiate it, and must remain involved.

For example, Ria and I were invited by CEO Jeff Kilgore to speak at Kilgore Industries, a large MEP (mechanical, electrical, plumbing) construction firm headquartered in Houston, Texas. Jeff is doing amazing things for and with his team. Leadership development wasn't new for him. He had been developing his team long before he discovered Blue-Collar Leadership®.

Jeff asked us to speak a full day on Friday and half a day on Saturday. Nearly 100 upper and mid-level leaders were with us on Friday and nearly 100 front line leaders on Saturday. Jeff was on the front row both days participating and taking notes. His "C" level leaders and other top leaders were also there. Not just on Friday, but they all came back on Saturday too!

"Leaders provide a mental picture of a preferred future and then ask people to follow them there. Leaders require those around them to abandon the known and embrace the unknown – with no guarantee of success. As leaders we are asking men and women not only to follow us to a place they have never been before; we are asking them to follow us to the place we have never been before either. That takes guts. That takes nerve. That takes courage."
~ Andy Stanley

COMPONENT 4
COMPETENCY

20

PREVENT ANXIETY

WITHOUT COMPETENCY, THERE WILL BE ANXIETY

"One source of frustration in the workplace is the frequent mismatch between what people must do and what people can do. When what they must do exceeds their capabilities, the result is anxiety. When what they must do falls short of their capabilities, the result is boredom." ~ Daniel Pink

The majority of the stress and anxiety experienced by those within an organization can be traced back to a combination of weak management and poor leadership. The actual job or work being done usually doesn't cause too much stress and anxiety. Not knowing how to do what is expected, not having the time to prepare for what must be done, and being expected to do too much too fast can absolutely cause a lot of stress and anxiety.

By weak management, I mean leaders and their team members struggle to effectively manage things and processes at all levels. By poor leadership, I mean leaders and their team members struggle to lead themselves and others well.

Remember, we're all leaders, followers, and managers. We all have a role to play, and we all have responsibilities at some level related to managing things and processes and leading people. Whenever people are involved, expect things to be very dynamic and very complex.

Stress and anxiety can be caused by a team member's leader who is a weak manager and/or a poor leader. The leader could also be a great manager, but a poor leader. Or, the leader could be a weak manager, but a great leader. Anxiety of this type can also be experienced when team members aren't able to manage their job related processes or influence (lead) their co-workers.

When it comes to stress and anxiety, there's a lot going on. But, it's the leader's responsibility to minimize stress and anxiety in the workplace. An organization filled with people who are suffering from stress and anxiety, regardless of the reason, will not become a sought after employer of choice because these people will be providing a constant stream of bad word of mouth advertisement. As they strive to release the stress and overcome the anxiety outside of work, they'll be bad-mouthing their boss and the organization for causing it.

As Ria says, "Fear is what happens when anxiety over something becomes overwhelming." Fear in the workplace isn't a good thing. Much of the fear may be unfounded. However, when we experience stress and anxiety, we begin to question our abilities, start telling ourselves stories, and start asking ourselves questions.

We begin to wonder if we'll be fired. We begin to wonder what will happen if we lose our job unexpectedly. We begin to wonder if we should find another job before that happens. We begin to blame the boss.

Poor leaders who manage people instead of leading them often choose to manage with fear and intimidation. Fear and intimidation will always cause stress and anxiety. There's no room for fear and intimidation in a high impact culture or on a high performance team.

Bob Chapman, CEO Barry-Wehmiller, made a great point when he said, "High trust businesses are built on respect and caring, not fear and anxiety." High impact cultures are built on high trust. Not sometime, every time.

To eliminate stress and anxiety, it's the top leader's responsibility to ensure everyone on their team at every level has the competency to do their job effectively, whether they're an entry-level team member or a high level formal leader leading a division with 10,000 team members. Competency leads to confidence.

When it comes to people development, high impact leaders do far more than is required relative to both character and competency. Good managers do only what is required in the area of competency development but neglect character development. And, low impact managers do less than is required relative to competency development and have never considered character development.

Many organizations introduce their new hires to stress and anxiety on day one by throwing them straight into the fire. These are most likely the organizations that can't find good people and "when we do, they won't stay." There's no introduction to the company's history, culture, purpose, or vision. And, there's no training related to what they'll be doing or how they'll be expected to do it.

However, I know of blue-collar organizations that train new team members up to six weeks before they're placed on the job. Low impact managers say, "We can't afford to do it." High impact leaders say, "We can't afford not to do it."

Different values always lead to different results.

"Sharing knowledge builds trust, and trust creates a culture of excellent performance."
~ Colonel Tom Connally, USMC (Ret.)

21

TWO AREAS OF FOCUS

CHARACTER AND COMPETENCY

"The ability to mobilize the skills and competencies of the people around us has a bigger impact on our performance than does the amount of experience we have." ~ Liz Wiseman

All leaders understand the need for competency when it comes to a person being able to do their job effectively and efficiently. I refer to competency as having the skill, ability, and knowledge to do the job. Competency will vary from job to job and organization to organization.

Most often, if you don't have or can't quickly acquire the necessary competency, you'll lose your job. Competency is a must for trust. If you can't be trusted to do your job, you won't be able to keep your job. Or, at least you shouldn't.

However, low impact leaders who are often struggling to find good people are much more hesitant about doing the right thing. They will often keep people who aren't a good fit, who don't perform as they should, or who can't or aren't willing to develop their competency. These low impact leaders believe anybody is better than nobody.

Most leaders accept the responsibility for ensuring their team has the appropriate competency to do the job. They may ensure a team member has it before they hire them. Or to be sure, they may conduct in-house training after they hire them. And, some leaders may do a combination of both.

Either way, most leaders will help their team members acquire the necessary competency because it's required of them. If the leader doesn't do it, he or she will lose their job. If a lack of competency development continues unaddressed across the entire organization, at some point the business will fail.

Developing your competency is a must.

However, developing both your own and your team's character is optional in most organizations. Most leaders and their team members develop their character randomly, not intentionally.

Throughout this book, when I mention personal growth, development, leadership development, or people development, I'm referring to character development.

In Blue-Collar Leadership & Culture, I'm attempting to motivate and inspire you to go beyond what's required by choosing to develop yourself and your team intentionally. When developing their team isn't required, most formal authority leaders choose not to do it. This choice is the primary reason so many leaders struggle to find good people and are unable to attract great people.

Great people already have a high degree of character, that's what makes them great. As a result, most often without ever sitting through an interview, they can easily and quickly determine if an organization is or isn't focused on people development. If not, they will not submit their application and will continue their search.

In the event they do choose to submit an application because they feel the organization overall is focused on people development, they will also be able to easily and quickly know if the leader conducting the interview is a student of personal growth and leadership development. If the answer is no, this great candidate will most likely decline any offer and continue searching for a great leader in another great organization.

Great people have many options. One of them is to choose a great leader. And, they know how to do it.

When there's a unifying purpose, a shared vision, and a defined mission, a high degree of character will allow you to convert your competency and your relationships into meaningful results and success for the organization.

Character is related to your behavior, soft skills, and values. Competency is related to your talent, hard skills, and knowledge. You must focus on developing both. However, you must develop the necessary competency relative to your job, because it's required. But, it's not the most important of the two.

Character is the most important because an individual's character will either maximize or minimize their competency. Ultimately, your character will launch you like a rocket or limit you like an anchor.

Stephen M. R. Covey made this remark relative to character and integrity, "Openness is vital to integrity. It takes both humility and courage—humility to acknowledge that there are principles out there you may not currently be aware of, and courage to follow them once you discover them."

In the previous chapters, I've shared a lot about "why to do" and "what to do." For the remainder of this section on "Competency," I'll shift my focus and help you learn "how to" develop the people.

> *"You can have great academic intelligence*
> *and still lack social intelligence."*
> *~ Carole Hyatt & Linda Gottlieb*

22

PROVIDE CONTINUOUS EDUCATION

MAINTAIN A LIBRARY
OF PERSONAL GROWTH AND
LEADERSHIP DEVELOPMENT RESOURCES

"Growth-minded leaders, they start with a belief in human potential and development—both their own and other people's. Instead of using the company as a vehicle for their greatness, they use it as an engine of growth—for themselves, the employees, and the company as a whole." ~ Carol S. Dweck

Let's now begin looking at how we can develop people. These methods will help you facilitate cultural transformation. These are not things you do once and forget. These are things you must do continuously to some degree for the life of the organization if you want to become and remain a sought after employer of choice.

The sooner you can start them the better. But, don't feel overwhelmed thinking you have to start them all at once. I'm simply introducing them to you. Do what you can when you can. There are also other things you'll discover and begin doing as you and your team grow and develop over time. However, the following are the primary and fundamental methods that will take you and your team to the next level and beyond.

Personal growth and development is an inside job that requires confidence, humility, and ultimately a desire to get better. As a leader, it's your responsibility to support your team. When you do, they'll support you.

The remainder of this "Competency" section is not only about how you provide development for everyone on your team, but more importantly, it's about how you feed those who are hungry.

By hungry, I mean they have a passion and a hunger for growth and development. They are bought-in and want more. They're all-in and wish everyone else was too. When it comes to real, sustainable culture change, the hungry people will be the tip of the spear. They will lead the way. They will help you the most, so you must be willing to support them the most.

When it comes to feeding the hungry, don't focus on title, position, or rank. Remember, leadership is about character development. Those who have the highest degree of character already and those with the greatest desire to improve their character will lead the cultural transformation regardless of their title, position, or rank.

The formal leaders should be leading the way, but often, they're not as hungry as those in the lower levels of the organization. The top leader should be the hungriest. But often, that's not the case. However, if they're fully bought-in, engaged in the process at some level, and willing to provide the time and resources to feed the hungry, they're doing their part. Most organizations don't have a top leader like this. They should, but they don't.

In 2005 when I started leading Lean Manufacturing where I was working at the time, the first thing I did was create an onsite library. I knew if I was going to lead a Lean transformation, I needed all the help I could get. I knew I needed to prepare to feed the hungry because they would determine how fast and how far we would go.

In my case, my leader, the plant manager, wasn't the hungriest. I was. However, he was fully bought-in, fully engaged in the process, and fully supported all of us, especially me. I started reading about Lean and Lean Leadership daily and continued for the following four years. I still read everyday, but my focus now is only on personal growth and leadership development.

As I began reading, I filled our library with the books, videos, and audiobooks I knew would be the most relevant. I encouraged everyone to check them out like a real library and to sign the inside cover, so I and others would know who had become familiar with the content.

The hungry people began to reveal themselves. When they did, I knew who was on my team, who was bought-in at the highest level, and who the hungriest among our 200 member team was. I knew I would be able to leverage my influence through them. If they discovered a book I hadn't read, but they wanted to read, I would add it to the library. It's great if others are reading content you haven't read. The key is they are growing. Do not limit anyone's desire to grow in any way.

I encourage you to establish a library, not only physically, but also digitally. Some of our clients create a library filled with multiple copies of multiple books and give them to the hungry without expecting them to be returned. Some create internal web pages with links to videos, audiobooks, etc. Some create a multi-level certification based on the completion of specific books.

Start filling your library. Learn more about our books!
Visit: BlueCollarLeadership.com/Store

"Anything less than a conscious commitment to the important is an unconscious commitment to the unimportant." ~ Stephen R. Covey

23

SUPPLY OCCASIONAL MOTIVATION

OFFER ONSITE PERSONAL GROWTH AND LEADERSHIP DEVELOPMENT SESSIONS

"We don't do a lot of 'awareness training;' we want people to be intensely impacted by their experience so that it leads to significant behavior change. For that reason, our shortest classes run three days, while long classes require an investment of two to three weeks. We want people to think differently about themselves and about their work."
~ Bob Chapman, CEO Barry-Wehmiller

Personal growth and leadership development is not about developing the toolset and skillset. It's about developing the mindset. A person's mindset serves as the lens through which they view the world. If you want to help people see themselves, their organization, and their future through a different lens, you'll have to help them develop a growth-mindset.

Bob's comment above is impressive. When it comes to building a high performance team and a high impact culture to support them, Bob's example reveals how the best of the best do things. It reveals not only what they value, but who they value. The Barry-Wehmiller team is many years into their cultural transformation. They didn't start out this dedicated. But, they have grown to this place intentionally and methodically year after year.

When you become a sought after employer of choice,

the Barry-Wehmiller or the Chick-fil-A® of your industry, no one can compete effectively because you'll be attracting and retaining great people. Imagine the word of mouth advertisement Bob Chapman's team provides him and his organization compared to a leader and an organization who doesn't invest in their team's character development at all. The difference would be night and day, and so would their results.

When you offer onsite or offsite development sessions, you're doing several things at once. You're demonstrating to your team that you're committed and cultural transformation is very important to you. You're demonstrating that you're bought-in at a high level. You're making them feel valued at a higher level because you're investing directly into them. You're providing new insights by introducing them to new people, ideas, and examples. And, if you're on the front row taking notes, you're humbly demonstrating to your team that you're willing to learn and grow with them.

Ria and I speak at small and large conferences and conduct onsite and offsite development sessions for all types of industries across the USA.

Recently, we spoke at the Architectural Precast Association's spring workshop in Louisville, KY. Those attending were either business owners or general managers. We were invited to present a half day workshop on my book, Blue-Collar Leadership® & Supervision: Unleash Your Team's Potential.

These leaders admitted they had never heard a message quite like the one we delivered. At first, most were a bit unsure and surprised by the character-based content. But, as time passed, they became interested. Most were engaged, buying-in, and nodding in agreement.

Like most leaders of blue-collar industries, none of

them were focused on intentionally developing their team's character and weren't sure if it would work in their industry with their team. However, one of the business owners fully understood and received our message.

Tim, owner of TMC Masonry and Northwest Precast, saw his role and his team differently. His mindset had shifted during those four hours with us. One of the last things we said that day was, "Deciding to do something and actually doing it are two very different things. If you decided to do something different today, nothing has happened. You must act on that desire." Tim didn't just decide. He took action.

During our session, we told the leaders about our "Special Offer" where we reduce our speaking fee to $3,600, provide 200 complimentary copies of our books, and pay all of our expenses to speak or train in any of the 50 states across the USA. Our message was simple, "If you'll invest in your team, so will we."

Within a few days, Tim contacted me. He explained he had been in business 40 years and had been very successful. But after our session, he realized he could and should be leading at a higher level. He purchased two of our "Special Offer" sessions and scheduled us to speak to both of his teams in Idaho and Washington.

He leveraged our influence to help cast his vision as he began to intentionally transform the culture within his organizations. We were onsite for four hours in both locations and helped Tim feed many hungry people.

Our "Special Offer" is subject to change. Learn about our current offer!
Visit: BlueCollarLeadership.com/Special-Offer

"The only thing worse than training an employee and having them leave, is to not train them, and have them stay." ~ Zig Ziglar

24

FACILITATE
TEAM-BASED INSPIRATION

ENGAGE THE PEOPLE IN THE PROCESS

*"The problem is most people overestimate the
importance of an event and underestimate
the power of the process." ~ John C. Maxwell*

Too many leaders believe they can provide an onsite development session for their team or send someone to a conference, and they'll experience major transformation. It simply does not work this way. It will not happen.

Attending a development event is like drinking from a fire hose. You'll get some of it, but you're going to miss most of it because there's a lot coming at you in a short amount of time. An event is a catalyst: raising awareness, provoking thought, and inviting reflection. As John C. Maxwell stated, "Most people overestimate the importance of an event."

An onsite leadership development session with us or someone like us is an event. A development event is extremely important. An event may or may not involve everyone. An event is motivating. An event is valuable. An event should initiate or support the process. An event is not the process. An occasional event will not lead to personal or cultural transformation.

At a development event, someone can do the things Tim did: have a mindset shift, increase awareness, decide to act upon a new idea, or do all three. But, to get to where I'm attempting to lead you, you must develop an ongoing development process.

The process must involve everyone. I refer to it as the steady "drip" of content, motivation, and inspiration which will lead to and sustain the cultural transformation. The drip is the opposite of a fire hose. The fire hose is full blast and intense with a short-term purpose. The drip is slow and steady with a long-term purpose.

I'm often asked, "What do the best organizations do to separate themselves from the rest?" They have leaders who lead their teams through book studies.

This is where team-based, team-facilitated, and team-led transformation occurs. It's extremely powerful, but most leaders overlook it. They think it's too simple to be effective. It is simple, but it's also highly effective. Reflect on the words of John C. Maxwell, "Most people...underestimate the power of the process."

Did you go to an event and become educated? No, you went through a long process. You're still going through it.

Tim not only took advantage of our "Special Offer" in order to help jump start the cultural transformation, but he also began leading his team through book studies. Although we shipped him the books right away, it was two months before we were able to conduct the onsite sessions. Tim didn't wait for us. He took the advice we had offered at the Louisville event and immediately began conducting book studies with his team long before we spoke to them.

Quickly, Tim realized he had made the right decision because his team was interested and buying-in to the concept and the content. Within a few weeks of arriving home after the Louisville event, Tim added a new member to his team to help him facilitate and accelerate the cultural transformation. Tim made it very clear to his team that he was bought-in, he was serious, and he was leading the way by investing in their development.

We teach a simple method for conducting book studies. Most of our books are formatted specifically for this purpose with easy to read, easy to understand, short three page chapters like this one. Preparation and homework are not required. You should participate too.

Assemble 4-10 team members. Make sure everyone has a copy of the book being studied. Select a chapter. The team takes turns reading paragraphs until the chapter has been read. Allow participants to pass if they don't want to read. While reading is occurring, participants should highlight points that interest them. It should only take 6-7 minutes to read the chapter. Then, allow each person 1-2 minutes to share the most important point they highlighted. That's it. Some clients do a chapter per day. Others do a chapter per week.

In 2013, we conducted many onsite sessions for an electrical construction company in Alabama. Jason was a front line crew leader. He bought-in and launched like a rocket. Today, he's in upper management and enjoys leading teams through book studies. Instead of having his team read, he plays the audiobook while they follow along highlighting key points. The key is to maintain the drip for your team. You decide how and when.

Download a book study script in the "Options to Implement" section! Visit: BlueCollarLeadership.com/Implement

"As a leader, and ultimately a mentor, you have the responsibility and privilege to grow those around you and help them become their absolute best."
~ Mike Davis

25

FOCUS ON IDENTIFICATION

IDENTIFY YOUR CULTURE CHAMPIONS

"When I first started coaching, people told me to put my five best players on the court. But I learned early on that this was not the key to success. It wasn't putting the five best players on the court that was going to cause us to win. It was putting the five players on the court who could work together the best. We won championships because we put people together. They weren't always our best players."
~ Red Auerbach, 9-time NBA championship coach of the Boston Celtics (16 championships overall as coach, general manager, and front office president)

The sooner you identify and engage your culture champions the quicker and easier your journey will be. These are the people who will help you carry the load. These are the people who will help you cast the vision and keep it top of mind for the entire team. These are the people who will read and learn much more and much faster than others. These culture champions can truly help you take your organization to the next level.

As you develop your character, you'll find it's much easier to analyze the character of others. You'll notice the little things people do that others overlook. These little things may be positive or negative. You'll also begin to better understand when it comes to people, the little things are often the big things.

If you purchase books to distribute to your team, be sure to give them this message, "When you read this book, if you enjoy it, value it, and are aligned with the principles you'll discover in it, make sure you follow up and let me know. Call me, send me a message, or stop by my office. I'm asking you to self-identify. I want to know who is truly with me on this journey. I need to know because we will be the ones who lead the way, transform our culture, and make our organization a better place to work. I want to know what you think and how you feel."

If you've never introduced formal personal growth and leadership development in an organization, you may be surprised who becomes a culture champion and who doesn't. Many of your formal leaders who you may expect to become champions, may not.

Those who prefer to continue managing people will do great harm the longer they remain. You must let them know you know they're not onboard. You must also give them extra support and time to change. But make it clear, the time will be limited and their participation in the transformation is not an option.

You should communicate the following to all of the formal leaders during the initial phase of vision casting. The higher up the organizational chart a formal leader is, the less time they should have to get onboard because their negative influence, negative attitude, and positional authority will send the wrong message to the rest of the team. They'll send this message without saying it, "Look at me. You don't have to change if you don't want to. And, if you don't, you will still have a job."

You don't want to leave them behind because their knowledge and experience are valuable to the organization, but when it comes to character and competency, character always counts the most. During a cultural transformation, leaders must choose to lead.

You may be surprised to discover many of your culture champions will be in entry-level or support roles. These people are frequently hungry for this type of change because of how their leaders make them feel.

Make your champions highly visible to everyone else. Make sure they know you consider them a culture champion, and make sure they know who the others are. What job title they have or how long they have been there isn't important. Being bought-in is what matters most.

I highly recommend doing extra book studies with your champions or allowing them to do them among themselves as a team. They're hungry. They'll be glad to do it, and it will accelerate their journey which will accelerate your entire team's journey. It will also allow them to form strong, meaningful relationships and send a message: When it comes to being a culture champion, it's more about the person than the person's position.

A strong message is always sent when high level leaders start conducting book studies with their group of champions. A typical team could look like this: a material handler, an engineer, a welder, an owner or CEO, a customer service representative, a supervisor, a director, a quality technician, a machine operator or entry-level person, a salesperson, etc. The key is forming these "special" teams of champions based on their current high degree of character or their strong desire to develop their character, regardless of how low or high it may be at the moment. Desire for growth is what matters.

Give your champions a reputation to uphold.

"A coach will call out the champion in you. They will see your potential. They will speak it over you. And, they will demand it from you." ~ Tom Mullins

26

SUPPORT
INTENTIONAL PREPARATION

TRAIN AND DEVELOP YOUR
IN-HOUSE TRAINERS

"When you invest in emerging leaders, it means you're serious about creating the future rather than just hoping it works out." ~ Mark Miller

Most often, when an organization begins a cultural transformation, they will need outside support. Ria and I help leaders select topics, develop a plan, and execute the plan by conducting onsite training and development sessions for various groups on various subjects. These sessions may be on leadership, personal growth, transformation, trust, communication, change, teamwork, selling with character, time management, leading process improvement teams, etc. We also offer limited professional coaching and mentoring to the leaders as they learn to lead at a higher level and encounter new challenges.

But, your goal from the start should be to begin doing all of this yourself at some point by leveraging your leaders and your culture champions. As they grow and develop, they should be growing with the intent to develop others. Developing others will result in additional growth for them while modeling growth for those who are watching.

When you're teaching character-based principles, you're more likely to become intentional about applying them yourself. Having others teach what they're learning will also accelerate their growth. We serve as models for our clients because we live what we teach. It's not just a job for us. The greatest compliment we receive is, "You both are so authentic," and we hear it a lot. We want to model authenticity for our clients because the key to teaching character-based principles effectively is to be attempting to apply and live them, at work and at home.

If leaders are willing to be authentic too, they'll be very effective at training and developing their teams. I highly encourage top leaders to get involved with the growth and development of their team members. Nothing will engage a team quicker than the top leader standing at the front of the room teaching leadership principles and humbly sharing their stories of success and failure.

People will always learn more from your failures than from your successes, so be sure to go heavy on the failures when you muster the courage and humility to train and develop your team.

Once you begin to identify your culture champions, there are various ways to leverage their value to the organization. Having them lead book studies is one way. Another important way is to ask them to formally train others on specific content.

Most often, the culture warriors are excited to be asked. No matter how busy they may be with their regular job, they will usually embrace the opportunity to train and develop others because they are passionate about the culture transformation, feel valued at a higher level, and want to help you and their team get better. They care.

Some may need very little training. They may be so passionate and excited to make a difference by helping others that they jump in and get started right away as I did. I simply started teaching others what I was reading and learning. My teams didn't expect me to be perfect, and neither did I. What was most important was that my team knew I believed in what I was teaching and felt my intention was to help them live a better life at work and at home.

To help our clients unleash their champions, we offer a lifetime license or certification to teach the content found in each of our books. Basically, there's a one-time license fee for each person who becomes certified. A separate license is also required for each different book title. The license allows the content to be taught to an unlimited number of people in various locations.

Each license comes with an eTraining kit containing a 60 minute video explaining the kit and how to teach the content, facilitator and participant guides, book study guides, and other related documents. You can also download the documents and print unlimited copies.

Learn more about certifying your champions!
Visit: BlueCollarLeadership.com/Certifications

"High performing organizations that continuously invest in leadership development are now defining new 21st century leadership models to deal with today's gaps in their leadership pipelines and the new global business environment. These people-focused organizations have generated nearly 60% improved business growth, reported a 66% improvement in bench strength, and showed a 62% improvement in employee retention. And, our research shows that it is not enough to just spend money on leadership training, but rather to follow specific practices that drive accelerated business results." ~ Josh Bersin

COMPONENT 5
EXECUTION

27

AVOID STAGNATION

WITHOUT EXECUTION,
THERE WILL BE STAGNATION

"There are three requirements for humans to act: 1) dissatisfaction with the present state of affairs, 2) a vision of a better state, and 3) belief that we can reach that better state. When just one of the requirements is missing, people will not act." ~ Ludwig von Mises

Merriam-Webster defines stagnation as, "a state or condition marked by lack of flow, movement, or development."

Development is the keyword when it comes to preventing cultural stagnation. This is why I've focused on development repeatedly. I want you to think about development as much as I do. Development should also be the word that's on your mind most when you finish this book. Without development, there will be no transformation, personally or organizationally.

Development is the objective. Development is most often the missing piece of the culture puzzle. Development is what separates great organizations from mediocre organizations. Development is what separates high impact leaders from low impact managers. Development, or the lack of it, will determine if your organization is consistently attracting great people or constantly searching for good people. Relative to culture change, lack of development indicates stagnation.

When it comes to culture change, development equals execution. No development. No execution. You can't do one without doing the other. When you're developing people, you are literally executing the cultural transformation plan. It's impossible to execute the plan without developing the people. It's also impossible to develop the people without executing the plan.

Peter Drucker shared these thoughts about planning and execution, "You cannot prevent a major catastrophe, but you can build an organization that is battle-ready, that has high morale, that knows how to behave, that trusts itself, and where people trust one another. In military training, the first rule is to instill soldiers with trust in their officers, because without trust they won't fight."

Development is what you should think of when there is an atmosphere of low trust among a team, in a department, between departments, or throughout the organization.

Development is what you should think of when you're frustrated or when you encounter frustrated team members, customers, or suppliers.

Development is what you should think of when you encounter resistance for any reason, but especially resistance related to change, process improvement, vision, and mission.

Development is what you should think of when there is constant confusion among your team.

Development is what you should think of when you become stressed or experience anxiety or when you sense your team is experiencing stress or anxiety.

Development is what you should think of when there's a lack of communication, people don't feel understood, tempers are flaring, and voices are rising.

Development is what you should think of when you

consider what it would be like to be the sought after employer of choice within your industry.

Charles G. Koch, CEO Koch Industries, commented, "Setting expectations according to general principles rather than specific orders not only helps employees understand the importance of their work; it frees them to think and innovate. We've experienced little progress when our people mindlessly followed instructions – whether they had good values or not." The goal must be to align your team behind unifying, timeless, character-based leadership principles.

Without continuous character development, your culture will become stagnant. Without character development, low impact people will not become high impact individuals. Without character development, low impact managers will not become high impact leaders.

When it comes to culture, if there's no development, there won't be any improvement. Culture development doesn't happen accidentally. It happens intentionally or not at all.

Are you dissatisfied with the present state of your culture? What should be better? Who should be better?

Do you have a vision of what a better culture would look like? Who will benefit when it becomes a reality?

Do you believe you can create that culture?

Did you consider your sales team? Don't forget them.

Develop your sales team with Mack's character-based-selling book: Who's Buying You? Until You Sell Yourself, You Won't Sell Much

"Above all, success in business requires two things: a winning competitive strategy, and superb organizational execution. Distrust is the enemy of both." ~ Robert Shaw

28

THE LEADER IS
ALWAYS RESPONSIBLE

THE LEADER IS EITHER MAKING IT HAPPEN (GOOD OR BAD), ALLOWING IT TO HAPPEN (GOOD OR BAD), OR PREVENTING IT FROM HAPPENING (GOOD OR BAD)

"Culture is owned by the CEO,
whether he or she admits it or not." ~ Edgar Schein

If the leader thinks he or she is not responsible for the culture of their organization, it's because they're a low impact manager blaming others, not a high impact leader taking responsibility. That may sound harsh, but it's simply the truth. I'm reminded of something I read as a teenager, "If the truth hurts, it probably should."

Relative to taking responsibility, Garry Ridge, CEO WD-40, provided a great example of what high impact leadership looks like when he said, "I am responsible for taking action, asking questions, getting answers, and making decisions. I won't wait for someone to tell me. If I need to know, I'm responsible for asking. I have no right to be offended that I didn't 'get this sooner.' If I'm doing something others should know about, I'm responsible for telling them." This type of high impact leadership above will lead to the same type of high impact leadership below. Remember, leadership is more caught than taught.

When I say, "The leader is making it happen (good or bad)," this is what I mean. When the leader does the right things, good things will happen. When they do the wrong things, bad things will happen. They may or may not be aware of the consequences of their choices. But, they're still responsible for the outcome whether they know what happened or not because their choice led to the outcome (good or bad). And just like everyone else, leaders can make things happen on purpose or by accident. Either way, they will always be responsible for the results created by their actions.

A leader isn't perfect and never will be. I know it. Their team knows it. We can only hope they know it. An arrogant leader, who thinks they're perfect, will create widespread distrust and have a tremendous negative impact on morale and culture.

When I say, "The leader is allowing it to happen (good or bad)," this is what I mean. The leader is allowing others to make good or bad things happen every day. Everyone expects leaders to allow good things to happen. When they do, they build trust. No one wants leaders to allow bad things to happen. But whether they know it or not, they do. And when they do, they create distrust.

General Colin Powell stated, "Leaders who do not have the guts to immediately correct minor errors or shortcomings cannot be counted on to have the guts to deal with big things."

When leaders allow something to slide that should be corrected, they are co-signing and silently signaling to everyone watching, "I've determined that choice or that behavior to be acceptable. Since it's ok for that person to do it, it's ok for you to do it too." There's no doubt, leaders are being watched. When leaders allow bad things to happen, they are negatively impacting the culture.

When I say, "The leader is preventing it from happening (good or bad)," this is what I mean. Leaders are preventing good and bad things from happening every day. Everyone expects leaders to prevent bad things from happening. When they do, they build trust. No one wants leaders to prevent good things from happening. But whether they know it or not, they do. And when they do, they create distrust.

When it comes to execution and building a high impact culture, leaders must become laser focused on making good things happen, allowing good things to happen, and preventing bad things from happening. At the same time, they should do their best to avoid making bad things happen, allowing bad things to happen, and preventing good things from happening.

Low impact managers get it wrong the majority of the time. High impact leaders get it right the majority of the time. What's the determining factor? The amount of integrity, character, awareness, and discipline a person has. Managers are more focused on what they're doing and what others are doing or should be doing. Leaders are more focused on how they're doing what they're doing, not doing what they shouldn't be doing, and ensuring others aren't doing what they shouldn't be doing. Leaders are aware that others are always watching.

Many leaders fail to execute effectively because they run out of time. Time management is really personal leadership. Has your team had development in this area? Is there room for improvement? Who would benefit?

Help your team learn to put first things first!
Visit: RiaStory.com/TimeManagement

"Every time you open your mouth, you create culture."
~ Stephen R. Covey

29

CREATE THE TRANSFORMATION

POSITIVE CULTURE CHANGE WON'T JUST HAPPEN; A LEADER MUST MAKE IT HAPPEN

*"If you want to start creating a Leadership
Development culture...then do the following:
Champion Leadership—Define and model good
leadership. Teach Leadership—Train leaders on a
regular, frequent, consistent basis. Practice
Leadership—Help emerging leaders to plan and
execute, fail and succeed. Coach Leadership—Review
new leaders' performance and correct their errors.
Reward Leadership—Reward good leadership
with pay, resources, and recognition."
~ John C. Maxwell*

The question you must answer at this point isn't, "Can I create a high impact culture and build a high performance team that will ensure my organization becomes the employer of choice within my industry and in my area of operation?" That's easy to answer. Yes, you absolutely can and should.

The harder question that only you can answer is, "Will I create a high impact culture and build a high performance team that will ensure my organization is the employer of choice within my industry and in my area?" I don't know if you will, but time will reveal your answer.

The determining factor will not be how much time or money you have. Those who say, "I would, but I don't have the resources or the time," are simply making excuses for why they haven't done what they know they should do. The determining factor will be your character.

High impact leaders will always find a way. Low impact managers will always find an excuse. When it comes to creating a high impact culture, those who don't make it happen will be left behind by those who do.

Cultural transformation is not about you, but it does start with you. You're the leader. You're the role model. More access to funds and resources can accelerate your team's cultural journey, but it's your character that will determine if they buy-in to your mission and vision.

No amount of money will make you: change your values, develop yourself, do the right thing, care deeply about your team, believe in your team, demonstrate respect for your team, value your team at a higher level, listen better, seek to understand others before you attempt to be understood. These choices have nothing to do with money and everything to do with character.

It doesn't cost a cent to change your values. It doesn't cost a cent to care for your team. It doesn't cost a cent to do the right thing. It doesn't cost a cent to express belief. It doesn't cost a cent to respect your team members. It doesn't cost a cent to make your team feel valued. It doesn't cost a cent to listen to others and seek to understand them. Transformation is an inside job.

However, it will cost you a lot if you don't do these things. Disengagement, turnover, low morale, low productivity, absenteeism, all come at a high cost. Not only will this high cost deplete the organization's financial resources, but it will also negatively impact your leadership team. The stress and anxiety levels, especially up and down the organizational chart, will also be high. High impact leadership is a choice, not a requirement.

I've provided you with a cultural transformation road map that will help you and your team begin to make your way to the top of the cultural transformation mountain.

You must start with **leadership development** of self and others which will reduce frustrations on all fronts, strengthen relationships, and allow you and the leadership team to more effectively generate buy-in.

When you generate **buy-in**, resistance will diminish allowing you and your team to move forward more effectively and efficiently as team members begin to align themselves behind the unifying purpose.

Once you establish and communicate the **unifying purpose**, there will be less confusion about your mission and vision and more clarity about who will be joining you on the cultural transformation journey.

As you help those on your team develop the character-based **competency** to lead themselves and others well, anxiety related to "Why are we doing it? What must we do? and How do we do it?" will diminish.

Once you transition from planning what must be done to **execution** of the plan, there will be no more cultural stagnation. You and your team will be moving forward. Cultural transformation is not about planning. It's about relentless execution of the plan.

Hope is not a strategy. However, you must have hope before you will develop a strategy. Hope is critical, but hope is never enough. Hope must lead to execution.

Everyone is not born to be a great leader, but everyone can become a much better leader. Everyone already has the ability to lead at a higher level.

"Create an organization that prizes the development of ability—and watch the leaders emerge."
~ Carol S. Dweck

30

CULTURE EQUALS CHARACTER

YOU CAN'T IMPROVE THE CULTURE OF THE ORGANIZATION WITHOUT IMPROVING THE CHARACTER OF THE PEOPLE WITHIN THE ORGANIZATION

"Culture and character are built daily, not in a day."
~ Mack Story

As I write this chapter, Ria and I are preparing to speak twice on "Becoming a Sought after Employer of Choice" to top leaders and business owners at the 2019 Towing & Recovery Management Summit in Washington D. C. There have been several inspirations for this book, preparing for these two sessions was one of them.

The event planner sent me an article to help me understand what the industry and many who will be in our audience are facing in the labor market today. The article was about a blue-collar business owner who recently went out of business after 41 years.

The owner mentioned he didn't want to go out of business, but he didn't feel he had a choice because, "It's tougher and tougher to get good employees...I love the customers, but it's just getting tougher and tougher...I'm tired myself. I've had enough." He also commented to the reporter that if he knew why it was getting harder to find employees, "I wouldn't be talking to you right now. I would've solved the problem."

Consider the owner's words, "If he knew why it was getting harder to find employees…'[he] would've solved the problem.'" This book explains the "why" behind his dilemma and provides the solution to his problem.

It's too late to help him save his business. However, I wrote Blue-Collar Leadership® & Culture for leaders just like him who really don't know "why" it's so hard to find good people. I would like to think if he truly knew "why" he "would've solved the problem," salvaged his business, and continued serving his community and the customers he loved so much.

But, I've also answered the "Why is it so hard to find good people?" question many times for many leaders across the country in all types of businesses and industries. As a result, I know that knowing "Why?" will not solve their problem. Knowing "Why?" will never be enough. Knowing "Why?" won't change anything but your thoughts.

If a person is overweight, they know why. They're eating too much and exercising too little. That's why. They likely think about why they're overweight a lot. But, knowing why and thinking about it won't cause them to lose weight. A person who wants to lose weight must know how to lose weight. Surely, everyone knows how. Eat less. Exercise more. Knowing "why" is never enough. Knowing "why" and "how" is also never enough.

We must turn our knowledge into action. Otherwise, nothing will change. Ultimately, it's a person's character that determines if they lose weight, not their knowledge.

I've shared many reasons "why" you should develop the people. I've shared "what" resources you can use to develop the people. I've also shared "how" you can develop the people. Knowing why and knowing how are no longer obstacles in your path. Now, you must act.

In the words of the business owner, "It's tougher and tougher to get good employees."

Solving the problem is tough too, but it's the right thing to do for yourself, your family, your team, your team's family, your organization, your community, your country, and our world. Many are counting on you.

Leading yourself well is tough. Leading others well is tough. Developing others is tough. Building a high performance team is tough. Creating a high impact culture is tough. Becoming a sought after employer is tough. Becoming an employer of choice is tough.

Few leaders will do this tough work. Many will stick to a strategy of planning, hoping, and wishing. You must do much more. You must commit to making it happen. Then, you must make it happen.

High performance teams are built daily, not in a day.

Cultural transformation happens daily, not in a day.

"Vision without execution is hallucination."
~ Thomas Edison

For a steady "drip" of development and growth content, follow me at: LinkedIn.com/in/MackStory or Facebook.com/Mack.Story

I welcome hearing how this book has influenced the way you think, the way you lead, or the results you have achieved because of what you've learned in it. Please feel free to share your thoughts with me by email at:

Mack@MackStory.com

Need help becoming a sought after employer of choice?
Visit: BlueCollarLeadership.com

ABOUT THE AUTHOR

Mack's story is an amazing journey of personal and professional growth. He married Ria in 2001. He has one son, Eric, born in 1991.

After graduating high school in 1987, Mack joined the United States Marine Corps Reserve as an 0311 infantryman. Soon after, he began his 20 plus year manufacturing career. Graduating with highest honors, he earned an Executive Bachelor of Business Administration degree from Faulkner University.

Mack began his career in manufacturing in 1988 on the front lines of a large production machine shop. He eventually grew himself into upper management and found his niche in lean manufacturing and along with it, developed his passion for leadership. In 2008, he launched his own Lean Manufacturing and Leadership Development firm.

From 2005-2012, Mack led leaders and their cross-functional teams through more than 11,000 hours of process improvement, organizational change, and cultural transformation. Ria joined Mack full-time in late 2013.

In 2013, they worked with John C. Maxwell as part of an international training event focused on the Cultural Transformation in Guatemala where over 20,000 leaders were trained. They also shared the stage with internationally recognized motivational speaker Les Brown in 2014.

Mack and Ria have published 20+ books on personal growth and leadership development. In 2018, they were invited to speak at Yale University's School of Management. They also had nearly 75,000 international followers at the end of 2018 on LinkedIn where they provide daily motivational, inspirational, and leadership content to people around the world.

Mack and Ria inspire people everywhere through their example of achievement, growth, and personal development.

Clients: ATD (Association for Talent Development), Auburn University, Chevron, Chick-fil-A, Kimberly Clark, Koch Industries, Southern Company, and the U.S. Military.

WHAT WE OFFER:

- ✓ Keynote Speaking: Conferences, Seminars, Onsite
- ✓ Workshops: Onsite/Offsite Half/Full/Multi Day
- ✓ Leadership Development Support: Leadership, Teamwork, Personal Growth, Organizational Change, Planning, Executing, Trust, Cultural Transformation, Communication, Time Management, Selling with Character, Resilience, & Relationship Building
- ✓ Blue-Collar Leadership® Development
- ✓ Corporate Retreats
- ✓ Women's Retreat (with Ria Story)
- ✓ Limited One-on-One Coaching/Mentoring
- ✓ On-site Lean Leadership Certification
- ✓ Lean Leader Leadership Development
- ✓ Become Licensed to Teach our Content

FOR MORE INFORMATION PLEASE VISIT:

BlueCollarLeadership.com
TopStoryLeadership.com
RiaStory.com

FOLLOW US ON SOCIAL MEDIA:

LinkedIn.com/in/MackStory
Facebook.com/Mack.Story

LinkedIn.com/in/RiaStory
Facebook.com/Ria.Story

LISTEN/SUBSCRIBE TO OUR PODCASTS AT:

TopStoryLeadership.com/podcast

Excerpt (Trait 3 of 30) from
Blue-Collar Leadership® & Teamwork:
30 Traits of High Impact Players

BE RESPONSIBLE

MAKING THIS CHOICE GIVES YOU A VOICE

"Total responsibility for failure is a difficult thing to accept, and taking ownership when things go wrong requires extraordinary humility and courage."
~ Jocko Willink

The higher we climb up the organizational chart or the higher we climb up the pay scale, the harder it is for many of us to remain humble. However, as high impact team players, it's our responsibility to choose to be humble regardless of our status or income. And if necessary, it's also our responsibility to learn what it truly means to be humble.

Humility is a choice that high impact players will make.

If you haven't accomplished much or done much, it's a little easier to remain humble. I believe as a whole the blue-collar workforce is naturally more humble simply because of who we are and where we come from. However, I also believe some who climb their way up from the entry-level positions let it go to their heads.

I want to remain a humble high impact player. That's on me. Not letting my success go to my head is my responsibility. I've also gone a step farther and made helping others do the same my responsibility. High impact team players always do more than is required.

Each of us is responsible for choosing our values and

those values will determine our circumstances and the impact we have, especially when it comes to teamwork.

Just as humility is sometimes a hard choice for those with a high position or status, taking responsibility is often a hard choice for those in a low position or status. But as I've learned over the years, taking responsibility seems to be a hard choice for many regardless of their title, position, rank, status, or income.

When it comes to teamwork, low impact players dodge responsibility like it's a deadly disease. They may disappear when the task is being addressed or begin to make excuses as to why they can't help and shouldn't be asked to help. That creates distrust.

High impact players know a secret: When low impact players are whining, it's easy to start shining. They also know how to shine. It's actually pretty simple. They just listen for whining, and then step up and say, "I'll do it."

At that moment, the high impact player builds trust by simply taking the responsibility. The next responsibility of the high impact player is to follow through and get results. If they don't, they will create distrust with the team and the leaders. If they do, they will build additional trust with the team and the leaders.

Leaders are ultimately responsible for making things happen. If they don't make things happen, it won't be long before they are replaced by someone else who will be given the same mission. High impact players know the quickest way to build trust with a leader is to help them get results, so that's what they focus on doing.

As they develop a reputation for helping the leaders get results, their influence increases with those leaders. Because of their choice (taking responsibility and following through), they earn a voice. As time passes, the high impact players are asked their opinions much more often than the low impact players.

As a result, the high impact players begin to influence the leader's choices and the team's direction. They're still on the team, but they're playing at much higher level. Those who are willing to make things happen are also given more chances to make things happen.

High impact players are never just along for the ride. They want to drive. They see the big picture. They don't shy away from responsibility. They wake up everyday looking for an opportunity to shine.

Imagine a team full of low impact players where everyone is dodging responsibility on every front. The leader will be frustrated, and the team will be frustrated. And little, if anything, will get accomplished. Unfortunately, these types of teams are common. Depending on your circumstances, it may be too easy to imagine this team. If so, don't miss what's right in front of you: endless opportunities to shine.

Now imagine a very different team, one filled with high impact players. They could be given the exact same mission as the frustrated low impact team. However, no one would be frustrated. The mission would be accomplished. Instead of being focused on finding excuses, the entire team would be focused on finding a way to make it happen. In that case, everyone shines.

What's the major difference between the two teams above? Attitude. Low impact players tend to have a negative attitude. High impact players always have a positive attitude. Attitude is a choice. If we can choose to be positive or negative, why not choose to be positive.

"Responsibility includes two important ideas –
choosing right over wrong and accepting ownership
for one's conduct and obligations." ~ Charles G. Koch

Excerpt (Ch. 5 of 30) from
Blue-Collar Leadership®:
Leading from the Front Lines

THERE IS AN "I" IN TEAM

EVERY TEAM IS MADE OF "I"NDIVIDUALS

"I'm just a plowhand from Arkansas, but I have learned how to hold a team together – how to lift some men up, how to calm others down, until finally they've got one heartbeat together as a team. There's always just three things I say: 'If anything goes bad, I did it. If anything goes semi-good, then we did it. If anything goes real good, they did it.' That's all it takes to get people to win." ~ Paul "Bear" Bryant

Paul *"Bear"* Bryant was one of the greatest college football coaches to ever lead a team of young men down the field. He was also a *"plowhand"* from Arkansas. A blue-collar worker. The blue-collar world has produced some of the greatest leaders of all time, so you should be proud and hold your head high. *Without them, the world as we know it would not exist.*

There's nothing holding you back but you. As my blue-collar friend, Donovan Weldon, stated so well, *"The only person between you and success is you. MOVE! The only person between you and failure is you. STAND FIRM!"* Those are strong words of wisdom. Donovan started on the bottom just like you and me. But today, he's the CEO of Donovan Industrial Service in Orange, TX near Beaumont.

Donovan's success didn't happen by accident. He made it happen. You can make things happen too! He's a blue-collar leader that believes in and develops his team on a regular basis. I know because my wife, Ria, and I had the privilege of being brought in to speak to his team about leadership in 2014. They are making it happen on purpose for a purpose!

It's time for you to stop playing small and start playing tall.

A college degree is not required for you to play at a higher level. Not having one is simply an excuse some people use to continue playing small. If you want a college degree, use what you will learn on these pages to find a way to get one. If you don't want a college degree, use what you learn on these pages to make it happen without one.

You are the key to your success. You must believe in yourself. You must grow and develop yourself, which is what you're doing as you read this book. Do not stop growing! And when the time is right, you must bet on yourself.

Understanding your role as a team member is another must. Those on the front lines often underestimate themselves because they can't see the big picture. They can't see the value they have to offer. Far too often, their boss isn't a high impact leader and needs a lot of growth and development too. Bosses are often given the title without any formal development.

When I write about the front lines on these pages, I'm not only talking about the people in entry level positions. They are obviously on the front lines, but they also have leaders that are on the front lines with them and various team members supporting them too. They can all learn from these pages.

This book was written specifically for anyone at any level that visits, interacts with, or works on the front lines.

The principles I share with you must be applied if you want to make a high impact and be recognized for leading from the front lines. Regardless of your position, the more you apply these principles, the more options you will have, and the more positions you will be offered as you climb even higher.

Teams are made up of "I"ndividuals, so there are many I's on every team, regardless of how many times you hear, *"There is no 'I' in TEAM."* As a matter of fact, *you are one of them.* Every person on a team is an "I" and has the potential to lead (influence) the team, positively or negatively.

"Leadership is influence. Nothing more. Nothing less."
~ John C. Maxwell

You must understand there are many official and unofficial teams in the organization where you work. They are very dynamic and constantly changing.

When most of us think of which team we are on, we immediately think of our peers, the ones on the same crew, in the same department, or working on the same job. This is our core team, but it only represents the smallest team we're on. We also support other teams too, as others support our team.

When we choose to contribute beyond our immediate team, we are choosing to be part of a bigger team. Often, this only requires a choice to do so. Your choice to get involved in other areas sends a clear message to the high impact leaders.

When you play tall, you choose to contribute because you know it will increase your influence and your impact on the front lines. If you want to play tall, you should want to be noticed, to be selected, to volunteer, to share information, to accept more responsibility, and ultimately, to make a contribution at a higher level.

As a direct result of your choice to step up, your influence increases. You're demonstrating you can lead from the front lines and will be seen and respected by all high impact leaders as a high impact leader. Your actions will not go unnoticed.

When you play small, you choose not to contribute because you don't want to do more. If your goal is to coast until pay day, it won't be a secret you can keep. When you make every effort not to be noticed, not to be selected, not to volunteer, not to share information, not to accept responsibility, and ultimately to not contribute, *you will absolutely be noticed.*

As a direct result of your choice not to step up, your influence decreases. Your influence on the front lines and with your leaders will be diminished. You are more likely to become reactive and frustrated blaming others for what you have chosen. Blaming others will further reduce your influence.

You first make your choices, then your choices make you.

"The most valuable player is the one that makes the most players valuable." ~ Peyton Manning

Excerpt (Ch. 4 of 30) from
Blue-Collar Leadership® & Supervision:
Unleash Your Team's Potential

UNDERSTANDING ARTIFICIAL INFLUENCE

THERE IS A DIFFERENCE BETWEEN SOMEONE RESPECTING YOUR POSITION AND SOMEONE RESPECTING YOU

"Into the hands of every individual is given a marvelous power for good or evil - the silent, unconscious, unseen influence of his life. This is simply the constant radiation of what man really is, not what he pretends to be."
~ William George Jordan

If you want to begin to lead beyond your position, you must be respected by those you want to influence. No one gives you respect. You can demand respect all day long, but it's a waste of time. I always laugh (on the inside) when I hear someone demand respect. You will never be respected because you demand to be respected, at work or at home. It's simply not going to happen.

Think about it from your own point of view. If there's a boss or manager you don't like because of who they are as a person, can they demand respect from you and get it? Absolutely not. You may respect their position. But, you will never respect them simply because they demand it. You *must* respect their position to *keep* your job. But, you don't have to respect *them* to keep your job.

A position will give you authority but not influence. Influence must be earned by first earning respect. The more you are respected the more influence you will gain. Everything I'm sharing in this book, *if applied*, will help you earn respect and increase your influence with others.

Having a position or title such as Mom, Dad, Coach, Boss, Supervisor, Manager, VP, President, CEO, Owner, etc. gives you authority and control over other people. I call this *artificial influence*. Artificial influence creates the *illusion* that you have *real* influence. However, if you choose to influence people using only artificial influence, you are not leading. You are simply managing. Sure you may accomplish a lot, but what are you leaving on the table?

You can easily validate the principle of artificial influence by considering those bosses you've had, or now have, that you would never follow if they didn't control your pay, your time off, your promotions, etc. If you only follow a boss because you *have to*, their influence is *not* real. It's artificial. And unfortunately for the company, most likely, you will only do what you have to do.

The title of boss is one that is simply given, often by another manager with artificial influence. However, when it comes to real influence, managers are not in the same league as leaders. If you develop real influence based on character-based principles that you have internalized, then you will *earn* the right to lead. When you do, those reporting to you will do much *more than they have to* simply because they *respect* you.

A high impact leader operates from a position of real influence, not artificial influence or authority.

Listen to the voices of those with *artificial* influence:

- How am I supposed to make something happen when those people don't report to me?
- I can't make them do anything. They don't report to me and won't do anything I tell them to do.
- I can't get anything done in that department. They report to someone else, not me. It's useless to try.
- How can I be responsible for their results when they don't report to me?
- If you want me to make it happen, you've got to give me authority over those people.
- My hands are tied. They don't report to me.

Phrases like those are always spoken by a manager, never

by a leader. I've heard them spoken many times in my career by managers who don't have a clue about leadership. The only influence they have at work is directly tied to the authority, *artificial influence*, which is associated with the position they hold. Without it, they wouldn't accomplish much of anything.

I remember being in a facility as a consultant once. I needed some help from a few team members in a different department, so I asked the manager I was working with if it would be okay if I went over and asked them for some help. He said, *"You'll have to wait. I'll have to get an interpreter because none of them speak English."* I said, *"Okay, I'll go wait over there."* I thought it was interesting. When I got there, they all spoke English to me. Leadership is influence.

Managers make things happen with people who *have to* help them. Leaders make things happen with people who *want to* help them.

Most managers have never read a leadership book and can't understand a leader doesn't need authority to make something happen. Leaders only need *influence* to make something happen. Leadership is *not* about who *has* to help you. Leadership *is* about who *wants* to help you.

Research studies have repeatedly shown a 40% productivity increase when comparing people who *want to* follow a leader with those who *have to* follow a manager.

A manager thrives on artificial influence and is not interested in developing himself or others in order to capture this massive loss of productivity. That's what leaders do, not managers.

How do you influence? What is your style? Are you a director or a connector? Do you tell or sell? What would change if you had more real influence in every situation?

"When we look at people who disobey their leaders, the first question we ought to ask is not, 'What's wrong with those people?' but rather, 'What's wrong with their leader?' It says that responsibility begins at the top."
~ Malcolm Gladwell

Excerpt (Ch. 26 of 30) from
Blue-Collar Kaizen:
Leading Lean & Lean Teams

LEVERAGE THE TEAM

FOCUS ON STRENGTHS;
DEVELOP WEAKNESSES

*"Instead of focusing on weaknesses, give your
attention to people's strengths. Focus on sharpening
skills that already exist. Compliment positive qualities.
Bring out the gifts inherent in them. Weaknesses can
wait unless they are character flaws. Only after you
have developed a strong rapport with the person and
they have begun to grow and gain confidence should
you address areas of weakness...and then those
should be handled gently and one at a time."*
~ John C. Maxwell

High impact Lean leaders have a gift for turning a group of people into a team in a short period of time.

At the start of a kaizen event, calling the group of people a team is a poor use of the word team. They are simply a group of people assembled in a room about to be given a task to accomplish together. Most often, some want to be there, and some don't want to be there. Odds are, this specific group of people has never worked together on a project before.

Knowing about continuous improvement is a must if you're going to lead a kaizen event. However, knowing about continuous improvement (your competency) will not be the key to turning a group of people into a team of people. Turning a group of people into a team of people is about having respect for the people. Your ability to quickly build a strong, functional team will be determined primarily by your character and secondarily by your competency. Your character is key in this area.

I've seen some very talented Lean leaders and others who have an extensive in-depth knowledge of Lean attempt to lead kaizen events. Most often, they struggle from the moment the event kicks off until the end. They know a lot about Lean but very little about leading people effectively. Why? Because their focus has been on learning Lean, not on learning leadership.

When it comes to growing, developing, and creating a new team, high impact Lean leaders know to focus on the team member's strengths in their area of competency and to develop their weaknesses in the area of character.

Each team member's competency strengths (what they know and can do), if leveraged, will launch the team forward. Each team member's character weaknesses (who they are) will hold the team back. This includes you.

High impact Lean leaders know there are always character issues. We all have them. A few of us are constantly working to improving ourselves, but many of us aren't. Focusing on character weaknesses is why high impact Lean leaders blend leadership development and personal growth components into all of their continuous improvement initiatives.

This is why I utilize the 20/80 rule I taught you in chapter 19. I didn't start using it by accident. I started using it by design. Until then, I only focused on leveraging the team's strengths. But, I hadn't been focused on developing their weaknesses. I'm sure you already know the root cause of most major problems that arise during kaizen events, whether with team members or people not on the team, is rooted in character issues.

The majority of Lean leaders focus only on the continuous improvement (competency) component of Lean. As a result, they provide no leadership in the area that will hold them and the team back the most, character development.

The reason Lean leaders do not address character development during kaizen events is because many of them are not addressing it in their own lives. In other words, because they are not leading themselves well, they cannot lead others well. Character development is always the missing link personally and professionally.

In the area of competency, ask questions and generate discussions to find out what people like or don't like to do. Don't assume they like to do what they are paid to do. I always have everyone introduce and speak about themselves before I talk about anything. I ask what their job is, how long they have been with the organization, what their previous job was, what their hobbies are, what they do for fun, how much Lean and event experience they have, and I ask them to tell me about their family.

The answers to these questions and the associated discussions allow me to connect and learn about their strengths. Then, I'm positioned to leverage the team.

"Humility means knowing and using your strength for the benefit of others, on behalf of a higher purpose. The humble leader is not weak, but strong…is not pre-occupied with self, but with how best to use his or her strengths for the good of others. A humble leader does not think less of himself, but chooses to consider the needs of others in fulfilling a worthy cause. We love to be in the presence of a humble leader because they bring out the very best in us. Their focus is on our purpose, our contribution, and our ability to accomplish all we set out to accomplish." ~ Alan Ross

Order books online at Amazon or BlueCollarLeadership.com

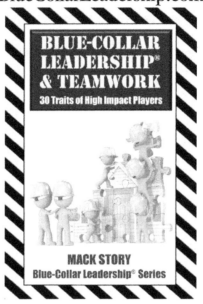

Are you ready to play at the next level and beyond?

In today's high stakes game of business, the players on the team are the competitive advantage for any organization. But, only if they are on the field instead of on the bench.

The competitive advantage for every individual is developing 360° of influence regardless of position, title, or rank.

Blue-Collar Leadership® & Teamwork provides a simple, yet powerful and unique, resource for individuals who want to increase their influence and make a high impact. It's also a resource and tool for leaders, teams, and organizations, who are ready to Engage the Front Line to Improve the Bottom Line.

Order books online at Amazon or BlueCollarLeadership.com

"I wish someone had given me these books 30 years ago when I started my career on the front lines. They would have changed my life then. They can change your life now." ~ Mack Story

Blue-Collar Leadership® & Supervision and *Blue-Collar Leadership®* are written specifically for those who lead the people on the frontlines and for those on the front lines. With 30 short, easy to read 3 page chapters, these books contain powerful, yet simple to understand leadership lessons.

Note: These two Blue-Collar Leadership® books are the blue-collar version of the MAXIMIZE books and contain nearly identical content.

Down load the first 5 chapters of each book FREE at: BlueCollarLeadership.com

Order books online at Amazon or BlueCollarLeadership.com

The biggest challenge in process improvement and cultural transformation isn't identifying the problems. It's execution: implementing and sustaining the solutions.

Blue-Collar Kaizen is a resource for anyone in any position who is, or will be, leading a team through process improvement and change. Learn to engage, empower, and encourage your team for long term buy-in and sustained gains.

Mack Story has over 11,000 hours experience leading hundreds of leaders and thousands of their cross-functional kaizen team members through process improvement, organizational change, and cultural transformation. He shares lessons learned from his experience and many years of studying, teaching, and applying leadership principles.

Order books online at Amazon or TopStoryLeadership.com

High impact leaders align their habits with key values in order to maximize their influence. High impact leaders intentionally grow and develop themselves in an effort to more effectively grow and develop others.

These *10 Values* are commonly understood. However, they are not always commonly practiced. These *10 Values* will help you build trust and accelerate relationship building. Those mastering these *10 Values* will be able to lead with speed as they develop 360° of influence from wherever they are.

Order books online at Amazon or TopStoryLeadership.com

Are you looking for transformation in your life? Do you want better results? Do you want stronger relationships?

In *Defining Influence*, Mack breaks down many of the principles that will allow anyone at any level to methodically and intentionally increase their positive influence.

Mack blends his personal growth journey with lessons on the principles he learned along the way. He's not telling you what he learned after years of research, but rather what he learned from years of application and transformation. Everything rises and falls on influence.

Order books online at Amazon or TopStoryLeadership.com

10 Foundational Elements of Intentional Transformation serves as a source of motivation and inspiration to help you climb your way to the next level and beyond as you learn to intentionally create a better future for yourself. The pages will ENCOURAGE, ENGAGE, and EMPOWER you as you become more focused and intentional about moving from where you are to where you want to be.

All of us are somewhere, but most of us want to be somewhere else. However, we don't always know how to get there. You will learn how to intentionally move forward as you learn to navigate the 10 foundational layers of transformation.

Order books online at Amazon or TopStoryLeadership.com

"Sales persuasion and influence, moving others, has changed more in the last 10 years than it has in the last 100 years. It has transitioned from buyer beware to seller beware" ~ *Daniel Pink*

So, it's no longer *"Buyer beware!"* It's *"Seller beware!"* Why? Today, the buyer has the advantage over the seller. Most often, they are holding it in their hand. It's a smart phone. They can learn everything about your product before they meet you. They can compare features and prices instantly. The major advantage you do still have is: YOU! IF they like you. IF they trust you. IF they feel you want to help them.

This book is filled with 30 short chapters providing unique insights that will give you the advantage, not over the buyer, but over your competition: those who are selling what you're selling. It will help you sell yourself.

Order books online at Amazon or TopStoryLeadership.com

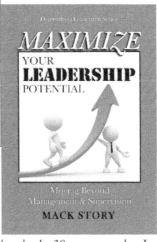

"I wish someone had given me these books 30 years ago when I started my career. They would have changed my life then. They can change your life now." ~ Mack Story

MAXIMIZE Your Potential will help you learn to lead yourself well. *MAXIMIZE Your Leadership Potential* will help you learn to lead others well. With 30 short, easy to read 3 page chapters, these books contain simple and easy to understand, yet powerful leadership lessons.

Note: These two MAXIMIZE books are the white-collar, or non-specific, version of the Blue-Collar Leadership® books and contain nearly identical content.

119

ABOUT RIA STORY

Mack's wife, Ria, is also a motivational leadership speaker, author, and a world class coach who has a unique ability to help people develop and achieve their life and career goals, and guide them in building the habits and discipline to achieve their personal view of greatness. Ria brings a wealth of personal experience in working with clients to achieve their personal goals and aspirations in a way few coaches can.

Like many, Ria has faced adversity in life. Raised on an isolated farm in Alabama, she suffered extreme sexual abuse by her father from age 12 to 19. Desperate to escape, she left home at 19 without a job, a car, or even a high school diploma. Ria learned to be resilient, and not just survive, but thrive. (Watch her 7 minute TEDx talk at RiaStory.com/TEDx) She worked her way through school, acquiring an MBA with a 4.0 GPA, and eventually resigned from her career in the corporate world to pursue a passion for helping others achieve success.

Ria's background includes more than 10 years in healthcare administration, including several years in management, and later, Director of Compliance and Regulatory Affairs for a large healthcare organization. Ria's responsibilities included oversight of thousands of organizational policies, organizational compliance with all State and Federal regulations, and responsibility for several million dollars in Medicare appeals.

Ria co-founded Top Story Leadership, which offers leadership speaking, training, coaching, and consulting.

Ria's Story From Ashes To Beauty
by Ria Story

The unforgettable story and inspirational memoir of a young woman who was extremely sexually abused by her father from age 12 to 19 and then rejected by her mother. (Watch 7 minutes of her story in her TEDx talk at RiaStory.com/TEDx)

For the first time, Ria publicly reveals details of the extreme sexual abuse she endured growing up. 13 years after leaving home at 19, she decided to speak out about her story and encourage others to find hope and healing.

Determined to not only survive, but also thrive, Ria shares how she was able to overcome the odds and find hope and healing to Achieve Abundant Life. She shares the leadership principles she applied to find professional success, personal significance, and details how she was able to find the courage to share her story to give hope to others around the world.

Ria states, *"It would be easier for me to let this story go untold forever and simply move on with life…One of the most difficult things I've ever done is write this book. Victims of sexual assault or abuse don't want to talk because they want to avoid the social stigma and the fear of not being believed or the possibility of being blamed for something that was not their fault. My hope and prayer is someone will benefit from learning how I was able to overcome such difficult circumstances. That brings purpose to the pain and reason enough to share what I would rather have left behind forever. Our scars make us stronger."*

Available at Amazon.com in paperback, audio, and eBook. To order your signed copy, to learn more about Ria, or to book her to speak at your event, please visit: RiaStory.com/TEDx

Order books online at Amazon or RiaStory.com

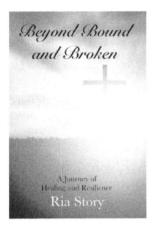

Ria's Story

From Ashes To Beauty

Ria Story

In *Beyond Bound and Broken*, Ria shares how she overcame the shame, fear, and doubt she developed after enduring years of extreme sexual abuse by her father. Forced to play the role of a wife and even shared with other men due to her father's perversions, Ria left home at 19 without a job, a car, or even a high-school diploma. This book also contains lessons on resilience and overcoming adversity that you can apply to your own life.

In *Ria's Story From Ashes To Beauty*, Ria tells her personal story of growing up as a victim of extreme sexual abuse from age 12 – 19, leaving home to escape, and her decision to tell her story. She shares her heart in an attempt to help others overcome their own adversity.

Order books online at Amazon or RiaStory.com

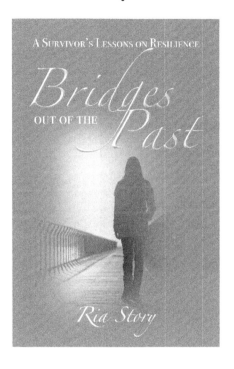

It's not what happens to you in life. It's who you become because of it. We all experience pain, grief, and loss in life. Resilience is the difference between *"I didn't die,"* and *"I learned to live again."* In this captivating book on resilience, Ria walks you through her own horrific story of more than seven years of sexual abuse by her father. She then shares how she learned not only to survive, but also to thrive in spite of her past. Learn how to overcome challenges, obstacles, and adversity in your own life by building a bridge out of the past and into the future.

(Watch 7 minutes of her story at RiaStory.com/TEDx)

Order books online at Amazon or RiaStory.com

You have untapped potential to do, have, and be more in life. But, developing your potential and becoming the best version of yourself will require personal transformation. You will have to transform from who you are today into who you want to become tomorrow.

Gain unique insight in, *"Fearfully and Wonderfully Me: Become the Woman You are Destined to Be"* and the accompanying workbook to help you: believe in yourself and your potential; embrace your self-worth; overcome self-limiting beliefs; increase your influence personally & professionally; and achieve your goals & develop a mindset for success. These two resources will empower you to own your story, write a new chapter, and become the woman and leader you are destined to be.

Order books online at Amazon or RiaStory.com

You have untapped potential waiting to be unlocked. To be successful requires us to have knowledge of the principles of success, awareness of how to utilize them, and discipline to intentionally apply them. There are no shortcuts to success, but we can travel much faster when we have an achievement model we can apply. This model will help you develop more influence personally and professionally, execute an action plan for personal success, and maximize your potential in life. Both women and men alike will find practical and relevant information to immediately apply to their situation and improve the outcome.

Order books online at Amazon or RiaStory.com

Note: Leadership Gems is the generic, non-gender specific, version of Leadership Gems for Women. The content is very similar.

Women are naturally high level leaders because they are relationship oriented. However, it's a *"man's world"* out there and natural ability isn't enough to help you be successful as a leader. You must be intentional.

Ria packed these books with 30 leadership gems which very successful people internalize and apply. Ria has combined her years of experience in leadership roles of different organizations along with years of studying, teaching, training, and speaking on leadership to give you these 30, short and simple, yet powerful and profound, lessons to help you become very successful, regardless of whether you are in a formal leadership position or not.

Order books online at Amazon or RiaStory.com

Become inspired by this 30-day collection of daily devotions for women, where you will find practical advice on intentionally living with a grateful heart, inspirational quotes, short journaling opportunities, and scripture from God's Word on practicing gratitude.

Order books online at Amazon or RiaStory.com

Ria's *Effective Leadership Series* books are written to develop and enhance your leadership skills, while also helping you increase your abilities in areas like communication and relationships, time management, planning and execution, leading and implementing change. Look for more books in the *Effective Leadership Series*:

- *Straight Talk: The Power of Effective Communication*

- *PRIME Time: The Power of Effective Planning*

- *Change Happens: Leading Yourself and Others through Change (Co-authored by Ria & Mack Story)*

Made in the USA
Coppell, TX
13 January 2021